PRAISE FOR
ENDURING THE CURE

"**A** powerful and compelling personal endurance through the unknown and into the light."
— *Joe Ebin*, president TurnKey Holdings

"**A** compelling, even harrowing, account of Carter's courageous medical journey. The story of her extraordinary resolve and the success of this remarkable new approach to treating multiple sclerosis dramatically demonstrate that stem-cell therapy can vastly improve the lives of those living with MS."
— *Janice Williams Rutherford*, PhD, retired, University of Oregon

"**R**achel Carter brings the reader step by step into her world of pain and loss of movement and control as this invisible and unrelenting disease (MS) progresses. Fortunately, she was poised to fight on many fronts. From her fight to find and see a doctor who could correctly diagnose her frightening early symptoms to her fight to obtain and survive the risky and expensive novel treatment to halt the disease. Carter's story will inspire others who face health struggles of their own. *Enduring the Cure* opened my eyes into her MS experience."

— *Amy Page*, MD

"**O**ne woman's story about her MS and the courageous step she and her family took to improve her life."

— Kathy Tiger, RN, SNP, LPC

"**T**hey say what doesn't kill us makes us stronger. Rachel Carter came to realize that to be true, but only after what was supposed to make her stronger almost killed her. A very personal story told with those who don't know multiple sclerosis well, but with a knowing wink to those who know it all too well. Inspiring, real, and very readable."

— *Trevis Gleason*, author of *Chef Interrupted; Discovering Life's Second Course in Ireland with Multiple Sclerosis*

Enduring the Cure

Enduring the Cure

My MS Journey to the Brink of Death and Back

RACHEL CARTER
With Margaret Godfrey and
Adrienne van der Valk

ILLUMIFY MEDIA GLOBAL
LITTLETON, COLORADO

Enduring
the Cure

Copyright © 2019 by Rachel Carter

Published by
Illumify Media Global
www.IllumifyMedia.com
"Write. Publish. Market. *SELL*!"

Library of Congress Control Number: 2019908575

Paperback ISBN: 978-1-949021-54-7
eBook ISBN: 978-1-949021-55-4

Typeset by Art Innovations (http://artinnovations.in/)
Cover design by Debbie Lewis
Cover art by Margaret Godfrey

Printed in the United States of America

DEDICATION

For Marin, Noah, and Hannah

CONTENTS

AUTHOR'S NOTE

I magine reliving the worst moments of your life. That is what I had to do to write this book. When I dug into the depth of the pain, I endured during the two years leading up to my stem cell transplant, it seemed unbelievable to me. I began to doubt my own memory. Could it have really been that hard? Is it possible for a human being to handle such unrelenting pain?

The answer is, yes.

Until the moment I met another MS patient at my children's school, I imagined my life moving from a walker to a wheelchair and, eventually, to a bed. My disabilities were mounting, and the quality of my life was sinking. The magic words out of that woman's mouth changed everything: "autologous hematopoietic stem cell transplantation." She went on to tell me that a doctor in Chicago was using HSCT to treat MS patients. I didn't believe it at first, but within twenty-four hours Josh and I, through internet research, went from doubting the possibility to relentlessly pursuing what we prayed would be a medical miracle. And it was just that for me.

This book recounts the worst years of my struggles with MS, the challenges of accessing the revolutionary

HSCT treatment, and the realities of enduring the cure. My hope is that my story reaches everyone who either has an incurable illness or knows someone who does. Whether it is MS or some other disorder, medical science is making breakthroughs daily. Although HSCT is not yet considered a cure by much of the medical community, I am living proof that it can halt the ravages of MS.

Although at times I almost gave up hope, my salvation was truly right around the corner.

☺ • ☺ • ☺

Some people have questioned my use of the term cure. Merriam-Webster's dictionary defines cure as "recovery or relief from a disease." What has happened to me does not entirely fit that definition. My recovery has been significant, but I have not gotten relief from all my symptoms. The progression of my disease has completely stopped, but I will always have holes in my brain as well as damaged tissue. It is possible for a brain to reroute itself, but there is no guarantee of the extent to which that will happen. HSCT halted any further damage. The degree of recovery is different for every person.

☺ • ☺ • ☺

I also wish to address my faith in God. My faith has been integral throughout the hell that MS sent me. As well as leading me to the man I needed to be married to in order to survive this, God also led me to the cure.

Josh and I met in college, where we were great friends. Just after leaving school we lost touch. We found each other and lost each other several more times over the span of nine years. Finally we got the message that we were meant to be together, so we stayed together. I needed him, and God knew that, which is why He kept bumping us into each other until we figured that out.

The person who told me about HSCT was introduced to me at the private Christian school my kids were attending. They were at that school because it was near a job I'd been hired for out of the blue in a field I was unfamiliar with. That job and that school were all part of God's plan.

A coworker at the job led us to our church in Vancouver. The church brought my family home-cooked meals when I couldn't cook for them, and fellow parishioners visited me in the hospital in Seattle during my treatment. They filled in the gaps when my own family was spread too thin.

I don't believe any of these things were coincidences. God had a plan for me, and I believe He does for everyone. My deep belief in this truth allowed me to take what, at times, seemed like an impossible leap of faith. My story is a testament that with God's help, nothing is impossible.

1

THE ME I USED TO BE

My name is Rachel, and I used to have an incurable disease.

That sounds impossible, but it's true. I had a form of multiple sclerosis, or MS, called relapsing-remitting MS (RRMS). The medical field does not yet recognize me as cured, but my story speaks for itself.

Defining MS without being overly scientific is difficult. At the most basic level, multiple means "more than one" and sclerosis means "scars." MS is a chronic autoimmune disease that is usually very disabling. Why people develop MS is not yet understood. MS is activated when an unknown trigger causes the immune system to attack an important part of the central nervous system called myelin. Myelin is a protective sheath that surrounds nerve cells and allows messages to travel through the nervous system. As the myelin disappears, the signals being transmitted no longer reach their destinations. The attacks on the myelin leave scars, known as lesions, on the affected areas. With continued attacks, the lesions can turn into "black holes," or entire areas of the brain that have been eaten away. By the time I was cured, my brain had accumulated fifty-five lesions and three black holes.

When I was first diagnosed, a doctor suggested I visualize an electrical cord on a lamp. In this analogy, the lamp is your body, the electrical wires are your nervous system, and the protective tubing or insulation wrapped around the wires is the myelin. When a lamp is turned on, the signal is carried by the electrical wires wrapped in protective tubing. This tubing must remain intact to ensure the current gets to its desired destination or your light won't turn on.

In my case, years of living with MS had left a large amount of my myelin—my protective tubing—damaged. I lost the ability to walk across a room without aid. My energy level was extremely low, and my balance was nearly nonexistent. At the age of thirty-seven, I needed to use a walker.

Walking wasn't the only thing I couldn't do on my own by the time I sought experimental treatment. I couldn't remove the lid from a jar, cut my own meat at dinner, carry my toddler safely (I dropped her more than once), walk up a flight of stairs, or even fold laundry. In fact, there were times when I could do absolutely nothing but lie in bed tortured by burning nerve pain in my shoulders and back. That pain made it impossible for me to work or take care of my family.

Now, amazingly, I face none of these afflictions. How did this happen? In 2014, I had a stem cell transplant, and it changed my life. This is the story of how that miracle came to pass and what that experience was like.

For many affected people, MS is an invisible disease. If you met me now you would see a vibrant, happy, healthy, successful woman. I appear completely put together. And on some days I really am all of these things. But I also have permanent brain damage from living with MS for fifteen years. Despite being cured, my days are still unpredictable, and there are times when I don't feel up to doing anything at all. Thankfully, these days do not come very often now.

When I was interviewed by the medical team before I started this incredible journey, they described me as "a pleasant, thirty-seven-year-old woman" who was "well-developed, well-nourished," and "in no acute distress." Even a team of world-renowned experts working on ground-breaking medical interventions in MS could not see my disease.

But there were periods when my disease was extremely visible. If you had met me during these times, my poor balance and irregular gait might have led you to believe I was drunk. I've spent most of my adult life being unable to walk a straight line. At the grocery store I would often stumble getting from my car to the entrance. At restaurants people would notice my husband cutting up my meat for me as if I were one of our kids. I needed help to put the lid on a take-out coffee cup. Being in this position was very humbling.

I think it is important that you know who I was before I was affected by MS. Later in this story you're going to have to envision me lying on the floor, crying and screaming while my devastated husband looks on. You're going to read about me needing to send my children to live with relatives. You're going to learn about how I used to take too many pain pills. You're going to see me in some very scary and compromised places, so it's important to me that you know who I was before MS defined my life. I am not the same person anymore, but the Rachel before MS had a lot to do with how I approached my illness and my treatment. She taught me to be fearless, adventurous, self-confident, and able to endure pain.

Without going into great detail, suffice it to say I had a very normal, healthy childhood. My mother was a teacher and my father worked for the U.S. Forest Service. My sister and I certainly weren't spoiled, but we never wanted for anything. Our home was loving and secure, and our lives were full of family, friends, and nature. It was always a given I would go to college, and it was during my college years that I began experiencing many of the twists and turns that shaped the person I was when I was diagnosed.

I started out life very shy. I was the kid who cried and hung on to my mom's legs on the first day of school. In spite of this tendency, I forced myself to be brave and try new things as I grew up. In grade school, I joined a community basketball team. I was the shortest, scrawniest, youngest, and least experienced player. It was intimidating, but I attended every practice and game. Initially I had a hard time doing much on the court because I didn't want to push the other players. I was scared of them. I eventually realized, however, that I had to make physical contact if I wanted to get near the basket. When I got my first foul my entire team, including the coach, cheered. That was when I learned that being pushy is sometimes necessary.

In addition to extreme shyness, my childhood was marked by terrible migraines. Before I was old enough to explain what I was feeling, I frequently experienced episodes of vomiting and crying. I wasn't diagnosed until I entered grade school.

Unless you have had a true migraine, it's hard to understand how disabling they are. I would wake up once a week with excruciating pain. I remember begging my father to cut off my head. Because the headaches occurred weekly, I operated on a six-day week. In spite of that, I always did well in school and participated in many activities. I grew up accepting that pain was a part of life, and I never used it as an excuse.

By the time I entered junior high, I was trying every sport available. In high school I zeroed in on cheerleading and was elected head of the squad. But still, I was a bit of an outsider. I was a country girl who rode a motorcycle to school. Instead of letting this bother me, I embraced being different. I was no longer the shy little girl hiding behind my mom. I was becoming a woman, in control of my own destiny—or so I thought.

My parents gave me a large amount of independence in my decisions, and I was in charge of choosing where I would go to college. I wanted to go in-state to get a better tuition rate, but I also wanted to get far enough away from home to feel I was on my own. I decided on a state college in a small town and, at the tender age of eighteen, I rode off on my motorcycle toward my first big adventure as an adult.

My desire for adventure grew from there. After my sophomore year of college, I had the opportunity to work in a fish cannery in Alaska for the summer. My roommate was from Alaska, and she told me that people could make good money doing seasonal work there. Now, bear in mind that I had been captain of the college cheerleading team—not exactly a fish-guts-and-sixteen-hour-work-day type of a girl. But I had torn a ligament in my knee at the beginning of my sophomore year, and I felt I needed a change after missing out on the cheerleading season. So I went to Alaska, where I met people from all over the world—and realized I had been nowhere!

I lived with my roommate and her family that summer and got a job in the fillet department of the local cannery. This was a case where knowing the right people and having a connection with a "townie" paid off. The fillet department was seen as a more desirable placement because it was one of the cleanest departments to work in and it required skill.

My crew at the cannery was small, and I got close to the people I worked with. The deep conversations, and especially the humor, made the unpleasantness of handling fish guts tolerable. We were all far away from home, and our crew came to feel like a family. We worked between six and twenty hours a day and then hung out afterward when we had any energy left. These coworkers were the most fascinating people I had ever met. Their stories introduced me to ideas I had never thought about.

One of the people I met that summer was Trent. He was so confident and cool; he had no inhibitions. He was not incredibly good-looking—he was skinny and had an odd-shaped face—but he was very charismatic and I could listen to his stories for hours. I was in awe of his carefree lifestyle.

Trent told me about a move he had made to Florida earlier in his life. When I asked, "Why Florida?" I figured he would say he had gotten a job there. In fact, he had had no particular plan; he just knew it was warm there, so he packed up his car and went. "I decided I would figure out what to do when I got there," he said. "I slept in my car until I found a job and a place to crash." He said there was nothing better in the world than taking a nap in the car; when the sun was shining, it got so hot that he would fall asleep effortlessly. It sounded marvelous.

I was amazed by Trent's story. It made me feel even more as if I had done nothing adventurous in life. I was meeting people from all over the world who had done things

I had never imagined. I got it into my head that I could do it too—drop out of school and drive to a new place, figure out more about life and who I really was. Why not? If Trent could do it, I could do it.

When I told my parents about my decision, they supported the idea of my gaining some life experience but were leery about the "moving to Florida with no job" part. As a diversion tactic, they offered me something irresistible: a plane ticket to Europe and Eurail pass. They suggested I live at home and work to save the money I would need to live on while I traveled. As soon as they made this offer, I realized it was a much better idea than the one I had stolen from someone else's life. I had my own life to live, and this was much safer—and even more adventurous!

I had never done anything like this alone before, so I talked one of my best friends from college into going with me. I had met Josh my sophomore year. My first impression of him was that he was a little dorky, but he turned out to be an incredible friend. He was just slightly taller than me, with sandy blond hair. I was attracted to his personality right away, but I wasn't dating "nice guys" at this stage in my life. He was the kind of guy who brought me food when I was sick. We both kept pet fish in our dorm rooms, and he would occasionally bring me a new friend for my tank. He showed his dedication to our friendship one night when I couldn't fall asleep. I called him and woke him up, and he got out of bed to drive me to the California border, fifteen miles away, and back, just to entertain me. At the time, I

THE ME I USED TO BE

thought these gestures were just signs of our friendship. I learned later they were more than that.

Josh seemed to be the ideal traveling companion for my European adventure. Not only did he speak fluent German, but he had lived in Europe for an entire year as an exchange student. He had been to most of the countries I wanted to visit, so I thought touring with him would be a great way to learn the ropes of bumming around Europe. When I asked him, he quickly agreed to come with me.

But you know what they say about the best-laid plans.

One week before my plane left for Germany, I got a phone call at work from Josh. From the way he said hello I could tell immediately it was not good news.

"What's wrong?" I asked.

"My car just got totaled," he said. I was speechless. After a long pause he continued, "I can't go to Europe now. It has to be fixed."

"But we're going to Europe," I said with panic creeping into my voice. "Can't you just fix your car after you get home?"

"No," he said. "I need to take care of it now." I was in shock. I continued to try to convince him that a trip to Europe was more important than his beat-up Duster. In my mind, he was being ridiculous. I was pissed. But after ten minutes of my trying to change his mind, it was clear the trip I had envisioned was not going to happen. I hung up the phone in slow motion and finished my shift in a daze.

I felt betrayed by Josh. I couldn't believe he would do this to me.

But the trip to Europe did happen, and it was exactly the adventure I needed. The time I spent alone in foreign countries taught me to be even more self-sufficient. It was also an awakening to find I was not really in control of my own destiny. Unpredictable things happen, both good and bad. Because I did not have a grand plan of what to see and do in Europe, I was open to anything. I listened to my fellow travelers and was free to act fairly impulsively. That is how I met Denise.

While staying at a hostel in Barcelona, I met two people who insisted it would be a big mistake not to see Prague. I spontaneously decided to go there next. The problem was that the Czech Republic was not included in my Eurail pass. I knew I didn't have enough money to pay the difference in my ticket, but I was feeling bold, so I got on the train anyway. This was a long, overnight ride, so I chose a car with only one person in it, a tall, thin African-American woman wearing a U.S. military uniform. I figured she was safe. She introduced herself as Denise, and we started talking with immediate familiarity.

When I told Denise about my dilemma of being on the train without the money to get into Prague, she asked me what I was going to do. "I guess I'll just get off the train at the last stop before the border and then walk," I said. Denise thought this plan sounded nuts and offered to give me the money I needed to get all the way into the city. I refused her offer. I didn't want to take her money, but she persisted. "My brother helped me out when I was younger," she said. "I always swore I would do the same for someone else. I had gotten into trouble when I was a teenager, and he took me in. I would love to repay some of that debt, and you need help. Let me help you."

We argued about it for a moment, ending with her agreeing to not force the money on me. After more conversation, we fell asleep. When I woke up in the morning, Denise was gone. I started to panic when I heard the guards in the hallway. They were asking for passports and tickets. I had slept through my last chance to get off the train without buying a ticket into the next country. We were crossing the border, and I was stuck on the train!

Preparing myself for what was coming, I opened my money belt to get my passport and Eurail pass out. I was frightened. I was in a foreign country; I had no idea what to expect. Maybe they would just let me through, but what if they didn't? The next moment, my fear turned to shock: my money belt was full of paper. I took it out to take a closer look. It was a mix of bills from across Europe, and some U.S. dollars as well. I couldn't believe it. I found a note mixed in with the money. It read, "Rachel, just pay someone else back. Denise."

My encounter with Denise was just one of many times on this journey that a stranger gave me what I needed to keep going. Whether it was money, advice, or a bed to sleep in, it was clear there were many angels watching over me.

If I hadn't been traveling alone, I doubt these little miracles would have come to pass or that I would have appreciated them as much as I did. I learned a lot on that trip, including that many things in life do not happen as expected.

With that realization, I forgave Josh for choosing not to come with me. I bought a postcard in Prague and mailed it to him with a message telling him as much. I did not want him to feel guilty for bailing on me when it was clear that he had felt he had to. His decision had given me a life-changing experience. I gained the confidence to live out the dream that had begun back in Alaska.

When I got back from Europe I jumped right into another adventure, working on a small cruise ship as a deckhand—but that's another story. After travelling to Alaska, going all over Europe, and working on the ship, I finally felt I had fulfilled my desire for adventure. I was ready to return to college.

Living in a large city offered more opportunities for employment, entertainment, and a diverse population, so I transferred my credits to Oregon's Portland State University (PSU). I had been a nomad for a long time, so having a home again was exciting for me. When I found an apartment one block from campus, I knew it was where I should be living. Not only was the proximity great, but it was also the exact same apartment that my parents had lived in when they had attended PSU more than twenty years before. This was a sign that I was making the right move. Everything was falling into place.

I got a job as a server downtown. The restaurant was a small place with one other server and one bartender. I became good friends with my coworkers and we went out almost every night. I knew every bartender in the area. I always gave them a friendly peck when I walked in the door and rarely paid for drinks.

During that time, I felt as if I had the best life ever. I had gone on three amazing adventures and had proved to myself I could handle all kinds of challenges. I loved my classes, I loved living downtown, and I loved going out with my friends. How could being twenty-one get any better?

I felt so lucky to be me. But once again, life proved to be unpredictable. My luck was about to change.

2

"I'M NOT SUPPOSED TO TELL YOU THIS . . ."

Looking back on the twenty-four years leading up to my diagnosis puts the time since in perspective. In some ways, that unstoppable Rachel is almost unrecognizable to me; she did not know the meaning of "slow down" or "I can't" or "no." I've had to learn the meaning of these words the hard way. In other ways, the young, exuberant Rachel still exists. Without the energy, courage, and adaptability of that younger me, I would not have been able to face the challenges that came.

Within just a few months of feeling like I had the best life one could ask for, my outlook began to change—drastically. I didn't know it then, but this change was the first symptom of the disease that would start eating away at my brain. Depression was one of many symptoms—some quite bizarre—I would soon begin to experience.

My depression was severe. There were times when I would not leave my apartment for days. I was skipping classes and calling in sick for work. This was all extremely uncharacteristic of me. Up to this point, I had been fun-loving and had worked hard at becoming a confident person. I couldn't understand what had changed; all I knew was that I no longer wanted to live. Somewhere along my exuberant, life-embracing road, I had taken a U-turn. Worse, it felt as if there were no way forward and no sign that it would ever get better.

I could not let this go on. Eventually I told my mom what was happening. She encouraged me to seek counseling, so I forced myself to find a therapist at PSU. After I disclosed my situation and my self-destructive thoughts, the counselor and I decided the best thing for my school career was to ask for incompletes in all of my courses and take some time off. I needed to figure out what had caused this change and how to deal with it.

I did some research about the causes of depression and what a person could do to address it. The one thing that caught my attention was the connection between sunshine and mood. Pretty quickly I diagnosed myself with seasonal affective disorder (SAD). Once I thought I knew the cause of my symptoms, I got an idea and ran with it: I was going to move from gloomy Oregon to sunny Arizona! I knew I needed a fresh start to get me out of this funk. I had a plan.

Fortunately, my boss at the chain restaurant where I worked in Portland had been understanding about my many sick days. He had experienced depression himself.

When I told him about my plan to move to the Sunbelt, he contacted one of our sister restaurants in Arizona. They had an opening for an experienced server. It was kismet—destiny. With a job in place, I could move to Phoenix right after Christmas. I was finally excited about life again.

As the stars were lining up for me to move to Phoenix, something very strange happened. While working at the restaurant one night, I suddenly could not read the buttons on the touchscreen I used for placing orders. I had to rely on my physical memory of where the keys were. It was odd, but I was busy serving and didn't have time to think much of it.

Soon, however, I couldn't ignore the fact that something was terribly wrong with my eyesight. At one point during my shift, I walked to the bar to fill a drink order. I knew there were two steps leading up to the bar, but I couldn't tell exactly where they were. There were holes in my vision. I was not completely blind, but I certainly could not see well enough to accurately interpret my surroundings. I was beyond freaked out.

Talking about this episode is difficult for me because of what I'd done the night before: tried cocaine for the first time. It was irresponsible, and seems crazy to me now, but after feeling bad for so long, I wanted to enjoy myself. My move was coming up, my life was finally turning around, and I felt celebratory. But now, as I fumbled around with holes in my vision, all I could think of was the word cocaine. Was what I was experiencing due to the drug I'd used last night? Whatever the cause, I needed to go to the emergency room. Of course, I didn't trust myself to drive, so I asked a friend—the same friend who'd given me the cocaine the night before—to take me. I'm sure he felt guilty and was also scared that the previous night's activities might have something to do with my vision problems.

When I got to the ER, they gave me blood tests, checked my eyes, and gave me a CAT scan: all normal. "I can't find anything wrong with you. You may have some new virus we haven't discovered. We'll name it after you if we figure it out," the doctor said with a little chuckle. He thought I would feel lucky to have a virus named after me? I was dumbfounded. I couldn't believe he could be so flippant about my symptoms, much less send me home in that condition.

It was now very close to Christmas, and I definitely couldn't drive. It was a three-hour trip to my parents' house. A family member offered to drive me halfway; then my aunt would meet us and take me from there. I couldn't imagine missing Christmas with my family before my move.

It was a strange Christmas. There was an unspoken sadness because this might be the last holiday I spent with my family for a while. My undiagnosed vision problem was also of great concern to everyone. But on the other hand, there was excitement in the air too. My family was supportive of me trying a new location. They shared my hope that I had finally found a way to break free from the depression that had taken over my life. While I was home, my parents and sister offered to make the drive to Arizona with me, which made us all feel better about the transition. I was not in this alone.

After I got back to Portland my vision improved, but I was finding it difficult to focus on packing. When my parents arrived a week later to load the U-Haul, they were shocked at how unprepared I was. Suddenly I saw my apartment through their eyes, and I was shocked too! I had been an organized person until recently. Now my apartment was a disaster and I realized how little I'd done to prepare for my move. It was humiliating.

Looking back, I realize that I was having my first exacerbation. An exacerbation is when symptoms of MS flare up. The holes in my vision (known as optic neuritis), the extreme fatigue, disorganization, and foggy thinking were some of my first symptoms of multiple sclerosis. I know now that the depression was MS-related too.

Even though the move was harder than expected, I found myself in Tempe, Arizona, just before the new millennium. I had chosen Tempe, part of the Phoenix metro area, because it was where Arizona State University was, so I knew it would be full of young people and fun. I was going to start the new century with a new life in a new apartment. We moved my belongings in on December 31 and walked downtown that night. We had heard there was a street party going on, but did not know the details. When Billy Idol walked onto the outdoor stage, I screamed, "It's Billy fucking Idol!" Unfamiliar with the singer and thinking the expletive was part of his name, my dad asked, "Who is Billy Fucking Idol?" My family was laughing together once again, and I took this as confirmation that Arizona was the right place to be.

Not long after my move, however, I experienced another bizarre health issue: Bell's palsy. Bell's palsy occurs when the facial nerves are weakened, causing the muscles on one side of the face to droop. I had no idea what was going on when I began to feel as if I were choking on my tongue. This resulted in another ER visit, where the doctor gave me the palsy diagnosis. The cause was dismissed as a pinched nerve. The doctor told me that Bell's palsy is fairly common and should go away on its own.

The palsy did go away after a few weeks. For a few months I was able to settle in and enjoy my new life in Arizona. But it wasn't long before I was back in the ER.

One night before bed, I noticed a very strange sensation in my arm. I called my mom to ask her if she had any idea what might cause something like this. She repeatedly asked me to describe what I was feeling, but I simply could not. All I could say was that my arm didn't feel normal. Looking back, I would now say that I had felt my whole arm—every millimeter of my skin, the muscles inside, everything. This is unusual. Healthy people are not acutely aware of the interior of their limbs.

The next morning, I woke up feeling fine. I hopped in my car and made my usual morning Starbucks run. A few minutes later, I turned into the driveway of my apartment parking lot and missed it completely. I was stunned to find myself parked on the lawn. I had turned into that driveway hundreds of times! How could I have miscalculated that badly? After navigating my car to a parking spot, I walked up the stairs to my apartment. Each step I took felt completely alien, as if I had never climbed stairs before. It felt very similar to the experience I had had the night before with my arm. When I got into the apartment, I tested my balance. I lifted my right leg, and fell.

After picking myself up off the floor, I felt a bit more normal and decided I could go to work. I followed my usual routine and stepped into the shower. As I closed my eyes to wash my hair, I fell again. The well-known commercial flashed through my head before I hit the wall: "I've fallen, and I can't get up!" Did I need a medical alert button? That's when I finally called in sick, called a cab, and headed again to the ER.

After sitting in the waiting room for three hours, I was finally taken back to an examination area where I met with a young, attractive doctor. He looked like the kind of guy who went for a five-mile run every morning before work. He oozed self-confidence. He diagnosed my problem as an inner ear infection. I insisted that there was a more serious problem and listed the multiple symptoms I had experienced recently. He was completely dismissive. "I see this all the time; it's an inner ear infection. There is nothing I can do for you. I suggest you see your general physician." I left the ER again knowing something was very wrong, but having no idea what.

The ER doctor's advice presented a new problem: I didn't have a general physician in Arizona. I hadn't needed to see a doctor except for these weird neurological symptoms I was plagued with, which every ER doctor had dismissed. I looked up doctors near my apartment and made an appointment with the first one who could see me that day.

I still felt like a jellyfish so, once again, I called a cab to take me to my appointment. I presented my string of medical issues to the new doctor who, almost on cue, said, "It's an inner ear infection." I had gone from a young handsome newbie to an older, more experienced doctor, yet still got the same unhelpful answer.

"It isn't my damn ear!" I shouted in frustration. He calmly recommended I see a neurologist if I wanted to pursue a second opinion. After mumbling "hypochondriac" under his breath, he asked his receptionist to give me a list of neurologists in the area. She warned me that I would not be able to get an appointment within the next six months without my case being labeled an emergency, and she knew the doctor was unwilling to do that.

By the time I got home I was exhausted. The receptionist had given me a long list of neurologists, but in my current state I could not summon the energy to call one number, let alone a list of them. But there was one call I knew I had to make.

With great trepidation and humility, I called home. As the phone rang, my mind teemed with anxiety and fear. I had made this move, distancing myself from my family's support. I was experiencing odd manifestations of an as-yet-undiagnosed illness. I had things happening to and in my body that I couldn't explain. Hell, doctors couldn't explain them!

"Hello?" I felt relief hearing my mother's comforting voice. The first words out of my mouth were "I hate to ask, but . . ." Before I could finish my question, my mom said, "I already booked a flight. I'll fly out tonight." I burst into tears.

My parents had already figured out that I needed help. I was never a whiner, so they knew I must have been in dire straits when I called the night before to talk about my arm. Without my knowledge, my parents had already discussed the most recent developments in my health. I had been having unusual problems for several months: vision gaps, Bell's palsy, depression, and balance issues. They already knew it was adding up to some sort of neurological ailment.

As my mom began throwing necessities into a bag and getting ready to drive to the airport, my dad turned to Google to begin researching. That was when MS entered my father's world. In the end, he would know my diagnosis before I did.

My mom showed up at my door the next day. The first thing she did was feed me. By this time, I had completely lost the use of my left arm, and my right arm had become severely fatigued. After listening to my story about the day before and ranting about the useless doctor for a few minutes ("How did that GD doctor think you could call all these neurologists when you can't get a fork to your mouth?!"), my mother got busy calling name after name on the list. She gave each receptionist the list of symptoms I'd had since before Christmas and begged for an appointment; no office had an opening. She kept trying, but I could tell she was getting worn down. Meanwhile, I lay on the couch listening while fear welled up inside. I felt entirely hopeless and helpless.

After two hours of disappointment, Mom finally reached an understanding receptionist willing to listen to her entire story. "Do you have a daughter?" my mom pleaded. "What would you do?"

"You need to take her to the Scottsdale ER," the receptionist told her, "and refuse to leave until they give her an MRI."

With difficulty Mom got me into the car. We made the hour-long drive to Scottsdale, which led to another long day of waiting. First a young resident took my information and put me on a list. Then my mom and I sat together in the waiting room listening for my name to be called.

The day dragged on. I fidgeted and tried to get comfortable in the waiting room chairs.

Eventually, I curled up on an empty gurney in the hallway. I don't know how many times my mother asked the ER staff how much longer it would be. It seemed endless. Finally, mid afternoon, a member of the nursing staff put me in a wheelchair and took me off to the room where the hospital did magnetic resonance imaging, or MRI.

MRI uses magnetic fields and radio waves to capture images of multiple layers of part of the body. The images are collected in sessions, and the patient must remain in the MRI machine for however many sessions it takes to get the necessary information. Some sessions last two minutes; others can last up to twenty. This was my first MRI.

The hospital staff put me on a table with a plastic mask, similar to a hockey mask, over my head and face. The technician warned me not to move; a patient must be completely still in order for the machine to get a readable scan. When the table I was lying on moved into the tube,

I felt as if I had entered a coffin. It was small, stifling, and hot. And the worst part was the noise—percussive rattling and banging that went on and on. They did several scans, lasting about an hour, before they pulled me out to inject a differential, or tracer, into my bloodstream. This would highlight any inflammation I had in my brain and make it show up as a white spot. Then they sent me back in for another half hour. I don't think I could have held still that long if I hadn't been so exhausted from my illness.

After the MRI, I was given a room where we waited for the results. My mom and I did our best to joke about the day and laugh; that is what our family has always done in difficult situations. We knew we were bracing for bad news. My mom kept scanning the area for the resident who had taken my information when we'd arrived at the ER. She assumed he would be the person to give us the MRI results.

The hands of the clock crawled by. I asked my mother how it could possibly take this long to get my results; we had been in the ER for ten hours at this point. Just then, a young female doctor we hadn't seen before walked in. I will never forget her short blond hair and light pink scrubs. I was frightened by her serious gaze as she spoke to me.

"I am not supposed to tell you this, but I don't think it is fair for you to have to wait any longer," she said. "The resident you met with earlier today is a chicken and clocked out. He went home because he didn't want to deliver your diagnosis. We have a neurologist coming in to talk to you. You have multiple sclerosis."

3

UNINTERRUPTED

I started to cry.

I did not know what multiple sclerosis was, but it certainly sounded bad. And if a doctor was too shaken to give me that diagnosis, it must be *really* bad.

My head was spinning with questions. Could I really have a serious illness? Was it terminal? Was my life over? What did this mean for my future? Why me? Even as my head whirled, I kept returning to the thought that it must be a mistake. I simply could not believe what was happening to me. Fear and anxiety began crashing over me in relentless, terrible waves.

While I tried in vain to pull myself together, my mom called my dad and put him on speaker. Based on the neurological issues I had been experiencing, he had already reached the conclusion that I had MS. While my mom and I had spent the day trying to discover the unknown, he had been online learning all he could about the disease. The three of us shared this sad and scary moment together. We now had a name for what I was facing—but did it really feel any better to know what it was called when I had no idea what it meant?

Mom and I reluctantly hung up the phone and went back to the agony of waiting. Eventually the door opened and a tall, thin man with glasses stepped into the room. He introduced himself as the neurologist on call. His face showed absolutely no emotion as he began explaining MS to us. He might as well have been explaining our cable bill. In the moment, though, I was actually relieved that there was no small talk. He must have known how anxious we were to understand exactly what my diagnosis meant. This was the first time I had heard the terms *multiple sclerosis*, *relapsing-remitting*, and *exacerbation*, terms that would soon become part of my everyday vocabulary. I don't remember much about the technical or medical information he gave us that day, but I do remember him saying, "This isn't a death sentence; you will still have a life. It just may not be the life you thought you would have." He spent a lot of time with us, talking and letting us ask questions and making sure we had all the information we needed to pursue treatment. He even shared examples of people he knew who had MS and who were leading relatively uninterrupted lives, dealing with the symptoms that came with the disease as they arose.

So there it was. I had relapsing-remitting multiple sclerosis. I was having an exacerbation.

Before he left us, the doctor explained that the most common and effective way to handle an exacerbation was to have an infusion of steroids over the course of four days. He wrapped up his explanation of my disease by saying, "The only thing you need to decide right now is whether you want to be admitted to the hospital and start the steroids tonight, or go home." If I went home he could arrange to have a nurse come to my apartment and start the infusion the following morning. After the day I'd had, my mother and I agreed that a good night's sleep was best for me at this point, and we knew I wouldn't get one if I started the steroids that night. He gave me a prescription for Valium to help me relax and sent me home.

☺ • ☺ • ☺

"I think it's too early to start researching MS," I told my mother the next morning when I woke up. She agreed. Neither one of us was ready to process new information. We did our best to engage in our usual banter over coffee, but we both felt a looming sadness and uncertainty about the near and distant future.

It wasn't long before the homecare nurse showed up. She arrived with an IV stand, a box of plastic pouches filled with liquid steroids, alcohol wipes, and informational brochures explaining the composition and side effects of the steroids. We exchanged a few pleasantries with her as she put the IV in my arm. After a short training session for my mom, she left us with everything we needed for the four days of treatment.

The IV itself did not cause any discomfort other than the quick prick to put it in my arm. The medicine, however, made me anxious and restless. My poor mother had absolutely nothing to do in my small, dark apartment other than feed me and watch me suffer. By the end of the four days, I was somewhat able to use my arms and legs. It appeared the steroids had halted the exacerbation. Over the course of those long, unpleasant days, my mom scoured the internet for something fun for us to do before she left me alone. She located a bed and breakfast in Sedona and made reservations for a two-night stay. I couldn't agree quickly enough when she said, "Now that that's over, let's get out of here!"

The last time we'd gotten in the car we'd been headed for a hospital. This time we were headed for a beautiful resort town in Arizona's red-rock country two hours north of Tempe. The landscape took our breath away, and our days there passed easily. We went to coffee shops and looked at art. My mom helped me feel so comfortable that I almost forgot about having MS. She always let me set the pace and rest when I needed to without drawing attention to my fatigue or making me feel as if anything about the trip was abnormal. It was more than just a vacation; it was a vacation from my diagnosis.

Because of those two beautiful days of recovery, I later gave my first daughter the middle name Sedona. I wanted her name to remind me of the mother I hoped to be—one who could make everything seem all right even under the worst of circumstances.

After the mini vacation, it was time for me to go back to my apartment and for my mother to return to Oregon. I was alone for the first time in over a week. I was anxious to get back to work. After I tried and failed twice to complete my regular shift, my manager asked me to stop coming in until I was truly better. He was very kind about it and assured me I would still have a job. "If you were my daughter, I would not want you working yet," he told me. "Just focus on getting better."

I took the rest of the month off, not knowing when I was going to "get better." During this break from work I followed the ER doctor's advice and found a neurologist. At my first appointment, I recounted my entire list of symptoms and told him what I currently understood about my diagnosis. This doctor told me that he didn't usually start patients on a disease-modifying therapy (DMT) right away because it was not always necessary and the therapies all have negative side effects. Given the frequency of my relapses, however, he was quite sure that I should begin taking a DMT right away. He started me on Copaxone, to be injected daily. That was the first of several DMTs I would take over the course of the next fourteen years.

At that time there were only three DMTs on the market. They were called the A-B-C drugs—Avonex, Betaseron, and Copaxone—and they were all delivered by injection. The A-B-C drugs became available in the 1990s, before I was diagnosed. Copaxone is administered daily and sometimes has a small site reaction, similar to a bee sting. Betaseron is delivered every other day and produces a burning sensation when it enters the body. Avonex results in flu-like symptoms for one or two days after the weekly injection. I would eventually try all three drugs, as well as many that would not be developed until later.

☙•☙•☙

It wasn't long before I took another fall.

A few weeks after going on Copaxone, it occurred to me that it had been a few days since I had left my apartment and my mail must be piling up. My unit was on the second floor and the stairs were daunting, but walking down to the mailbox seemed to go okay. I did not fall; I did not even stumble. It was exhausting, but I was feeling quite good about my ability to navigate stairs.

After making the climb back up, however, I opened the door to my apartment, took one step inside, and was baffled to find myself on the floor. I hadn't tripped or lost my balance; I had just face-planted for no apparent reason. When I tried to get up I realized I could not move my right side at all. Unlike the other episodes, this time half of my entire body had gone dead. I was terrified, and I knew I needed help. I managed to do some sort of army crawl with half of my body to get to the phone, but I had no idea who to call. There was no point in calling my parents; they were over a thousand miles away.

I did a brain search for somebody close by, and landed on Tim. I had met Tim just recently, but he seemed friendly and kind and his apartment was only a few blocks away. When I called, he picked up his phone right away and I explained my predicament. When I told him I needed to get to the ER he didn't ask any questions. He just showed up to help. I had called the right person.

By the time Tim got to my door, I had regained some use of my right side and I was able to walk to the car by myself, but I still thought it was a good idea to see a doctor. When we arrived at the ER and I described to the physician what had happened, I could tell Tim was alarmed. "You didn't tell me you couldn't use your legs. I would have gotten you a wheelchair," he said in a hushed voice. While the doctor continued to ask me more questions, Tim picked up my cell phone. I looked at him quizzically, and he told me he was calling my mother. He remained on the phone with my parents for quite some time, relaying everything the doctor was saying.

Unfortunately, nothing I heard at the ER that day was helpful. The on-call physician said that because the episode lasted an hour and not a few weeks, it couldn't be attributed to MS. He thought it sounded more like a stroke. After a barrage of testing, though, he was not able to explain what I had experienced. I knew that my loss of mobility that day was MS related. And I was learning that I knew my body better than a typical ER doctor.

This was the first of many times I experienced MS symptoms that a doctor didn't attribute to the disease. MS affects everyone differently. Just because a symptom hasn't been documented frequently enough for every doctor to know about it does not mean that it isn't an MS symptom. It just means it is not well known. Over the years I have heard countless similar stories from other people with MS.

My experience that day made realize I could not live this far from my family. I hadn't been on my own for even a year, but I was scared. I didn't know how this disease would alter my life, but I knew that when it did I didn't want to be

a plane ride away from my parents. I decided to move back
to Portland.

☉•☉•☉

Shortly after I moved back to Oregon, my old friend
Josh called me—the same Josh who was supposed to have
gone to Europe with me. This was a surprise. The last time
I'd spoken to him our conversation had ended on a sour
note. Through the many years I had known Josh, I had
suspected he liked me more than I liked him. We even tried
dating after I returned from my work on the cruise ship. We
had always gotten along well as friends, but dating did not
work. The fact that he called me every evening made me feel
he was too needy. I was still all about myself at that time; I
had no time for a man who "needed" me.

But when he called this time, I was delighted to hear his
voice and to find out that he had moved back to Oregon as
well. I asked him to meet me at a bar in downtown Portland
where I had started meeting up with a group of friends every
Monday night to watch *Joe Millionaire*. When Josh arrived, I
jumped up and hugged him. We drank, talked, and laughed
for hours. To my surprise I found myself flirting with him.

Josh and I had been in and out of touch—and in and
out of each other's favor—over the years, but we kept coming
back together. Until this night, I had viewed him as a young
and rather innocent boy. When we met now, however, I saw
he was not that boy anymore. He had grown up. I found him
funny, charming, and smart. It didn't take long for me to fall

in love with him. We had nine long years of solid friendship behind us, so the shift to love was pretty seamless.

Four months later we were engaged, and four months after that we were married. Josh did not focus on the fact that I had MS. He focused on me as a person. I asked him over and over if he was positive he could deal with the unknown future of living with my MS, and he always said yes. This was the man I was meant to be with.

Even though everything happened quickly, I did not worry. Josh and I had known each other for nine years. He loved me, and would forever. God knew this, and kept bringing us back together. I needed to be with a man like Josh in order to get through what was coming later in my life. His approach to most of life is to research and make decisions accordingly, so I knew he was not entering into our marriage uninformed. Having him as a partner in researching all the medical advances and discoveries in treating MS allowed me to live with less anxiety. I began to focus less on my disease and more on building a family and a career.

Things fell into place for us right away. I finished my bachelor's degree and got a good job. Josh completed his MBA and landed a job at Nike. We bought a house and had three beautiful children: Marin Sedona, Noah Michael Louis, and Hannah Grace. We were an all-American family. I began to believe the ER neurologist. My life *was* uninterrupted. Seamless. Complete.

Life went on like this for twelve years. And then, it didn't.

4

ONE MORE STEP

The majority of people with multiple sclerosis are diagnosed with relapsing-remitting MS, or RRMS, which was my diagnosis. Most people with RRMS eventually transition to secondary-progressive MS, or SPMS. In SPMS, symptoms worsen steadily over time, with or without relapses (exacerbations) and remissions. (There are also two less common forms, progressive-relapsing and primary-progressive, but they are not part of my story.)

Between 2000 and 2012, my disease had been manageable. There were even periods when I could forget that I had a neurological illness. But in 2012, my symptoms began to increase measurably. I feared I was moving into SPMS.

As my health became shakier, I needed to find a silver lining in this disease. I knew I was not alone in my struggles, so my silver lining became sharing my journey on social media. It felt good to know I could help other people who were in the same situation. I started a blog and named it

"Multiple Sclerosis Motivates." Here are my thoughts from a post from the fall of 2013 about how I approached the changes in my mobility:

One of the things I have learned—and that has helped me explain my experience to other people—is that there are multiple levels of disability for those of us with MS. As with many things that are hard for me to understand or accept, I decided to name these levels.

The first level I call "Think." The Think level comes right after diagnosis, before you really have any disability. You think about what might happen, what the future might look like, and you research the heck out of this disease that suddenly explains all the weird symptoms so many doctors have told you to ignore. It's an ironic name for me to choose, actually, because after I was diagnosed I didn't know what to think. I knew I should be distressed and aware of my body, but that was about all I knew. Frankly, I tried <u>not</u> to think about it.

"Live" is the second level. During the Live period, you know what MS is; you know what can happen—and it does from time to time. But the exacerbations that happen during Live rarely have major lasting effects, and the recovery is relatively quick. In this stage you live a very normal life. You may make some lifestyle changes, as I did. I started eating healthier, and I

quit bad habits like staying up all night. I ran two marathons, several half marathons, and I lifted weights in the morning before work. I quit eating gluten and I started juicing, all to give myself the best chance at reducing the harm the lesions on my brain might cause. In my case, I spent twelve years in Live, believing these lifestyle changes had worked. I would come to find out otherwise.

For most people with MS, Live eventually gives way to "Reality." In this level you are forced to accept that you are losing abilities and experiencing limitations that are most likely permanent. This is when you get really serious about hanging on to the mobility and stability you have and staying as positive as possible. You learn tricks to keep yourself working out: working out first thing in the morning, or decreasing the intensity of the workouts. You set up resources to help yourself deal with all the emotional fallout. You learn how to make things more efficient in your house.

At the point when things really became unbearable, I knew I had moved to level four: "Hybrid." In Hybrid you start needing assistance with simple tasks, like putting a lid on a paper coffee cup. In Hybrid the fatigue is so extreme you don't always make it through a day at work, if you make it to work at all. You can walk only a limited distance without a rest; for me half a block was all I could manage. In Hybrid I was using a walker at work and requesting a wheelchair at the airport. I learned once again how to accept a new situation—one somewhere between a life of compromise and support on one hand, and total dependence on the other.

Putting names to these levels allowed me see where I stood on the slope of my decline. Once I pictured and acknowledged it, I could stop crying and accept that where I was was just another chapter. Luckily, I've never had to name level five.

☙ • ☙ • ☙

By the beginning of 2007, I was at level two, Live. I had experienced some exacerbations, but mostly I was a fully functioning person. No one would guess I had MS. In fact, I didn't tell most people, and if it did come up, they were shocked. I was a busy wife and mom with a full-time job as a salesperson at a wood production mill. I went to church, worked out, and jogged twenty to thirty miles a week.

Running had become an important part of my life in the years after my diagnosis. Running became how I meditated; it kept me centered. Running helped me solidify the traits I would desperately need to deal with this disease. It taught me to not give up when I got tired. It taught me to mentally push myself past the point of comfort. As long as I was determined, I could reach my goals. While training for my first race, I adopted the mantra "one more step." I have used that mantra for every challenge I have encountered since.

I got serious about running in February of 2007. I was at work one day when one of my favorite customers called me. "You run, right?" he asked me. "You should do the Robie Creek Half with me!"

Robie Creek is the site of an annual half marathon in Boise, Idaho. I had never run anything close to thirteen miles before; at the time I was running only two or three miles at a time. But my customer sounded so excited about training and running the race as a team that I impulsively said yes. I enjoyed a good challenge and was easily persuaded. Of course I could run a half marathon—I could do anything!

The day after that phone call I started training. The Robie Creek race is not just any half marathon; it is known as the toughest in the Northwest. In fact, many runners say that this particular half marathon is as hard as a full one. The first eight miles are uphill, gaining two thousand feet in altitude. To prepare for this I had to start a rigorous training schedule. The first day I ran three miles. It was hard. *Really* hard. That was when my body reminded me that I had MS. Could I run thirteen miles? Take the facts that I was not a natural runner and I was over thirty, and then add MS to the equation. Could I run that far and push myself that hard?

As my training schedule got more intense, I started to doubt my ability to complete the race. Soon, though, I felt I no longer had a choice. Not only had I made a commitment to my customer, I had also tried to convince everyone in my company to do it with me! I couldn't back out now. I ran every day. When it got hard, I told myself I would go just one more step for as long as I could or until I reached my goal for the day. The miraculous thing was that I kept reaching my goals! When I passed five miles and I felt as if I might die, I was still able to go one more step—until I got to six miles, and then seven, and then eight. I couldn't believe it!

I knew it would be wise to have a few shorter practice races under my belt. My first race was a 15K (about nine miles). It was in my home town and fit into my training schedule perfectly. It was also mostly uphill, which was ideal for my training. Halfway through the race, I didn't think I was going to make it. Everything hurt, and it felt impossible to keep going. Negative thoughts started creeping in like nasty little parasites. I started thinking about how I had it worse than the other runners in the race. I was more tired than they were. They would make it to the finish line and I wouldn't. I had MS and they didn't. It wasn't fair!

When I caught myself indulging in these negative thoughts, a change washed over me. Right then and there, I vowed I would not let this disease get in my way. I started listing my advantages. I knew I could push myself harder than the other runners could. I could get through what most people could not. I had experienced things they could not imagine and I had kept moving forward. I could do this too.

I could go one more step. I knew what it felt like to lose the ability to walk. I remembered falling to the floor in a panic. I was lucky enough to get better after each exacerbation. This was what I thought about as I finished that first race— one more step at a time.

I did run the Robie Creek half marathon, and I kept on running—five half and two full marathons. I was never the fastest, but I won every time just by finishing.

◉•◉•◉

Even after I was no longer training for marathons I still ran every day. One of the many things I loved about my job was its location on the Columbia River. On my lunch break I would run along the dike that followed the river, starting just south of the mill. I could usually manage to change in and out of my running clothes and fit in about four miles on my hour-long lunch break.

Running on that dike felt like the perfect place to be, especially when it was sunny. It allowed me to escape from the stresses of work, and it allowed me to get completely out of my head. It was my oasis. I prayed sometimes, and sometimes I thought about the good things in life. Other times I just shut off my brain and took in the nature surrounding me.

Running was such a joy and a release for me that I took my Nikes with me when we went on vacation to Hawaii later that year. I decided to take a run on the path along the beach. Lava rock jutted up from parts of the path, sharp and pointy. As I turned around to loop back to the hotel, I tripped over one piece of protruding lava and landed on another. I walked the rest of the way back with blood flowing down my leg.

I didn't think much of this at the time. I had tripped over something sticking out of the ground; it could happen to anyone. After I returned home, however, more falls began to happen. This was the first symptom that affected me on a regular basis; my proprioception, or the way I perceived my body in space, was compromised. I was no longer able to reliably gauge where my body was. Eventually, after coming home several times with bloody knees and having to call Josh to come pick me up from runs when I had a bad fall, I was afraid to run on trails at all—even on my beloved dike. For a while I ran only on treadmills. But eventually even that became impossible.

My problems with proprioception were not the only issues plaguing me by the end of 2012. I had also started experiencing a tremor in my hands, which made putting pen to paper a real challenge. I was never known for my good handwriting; in fact my coworkers would tease me about it. But once I developed the tremor it was no longer a joke. When I was tired, my handwriting was completely illegible. No one could read what I had written, not even me.

I could not cut my own food at meals. This was especially embarrassing in restaurants, but even at home I hated handing my plate to my husband for this simple task. I had difficulty buttering a slice of bread or pouring milk. I also started dropping things. I simply could not coordinate both of my hands to do what I needed them to.

Eventually, I couldn't exercise anymore. Most of the time I couldn't even make it up the stairs to the bedroom without resting halfway. Stairs became my nemesis. My office building had a flight of stairs, and when I got to the top I had to stop and let my legs recover. They hurt so badly it felt as if I had just done a hundred squats with weights. People started to notice my limited mobility.

In the course of only two years, I had exited the Live stage and moved right through Reality into Hybrid. "Do Anything" Rachel was a distant memory. I could no longer tell myself to take one more step and feel confident that I could do it—or that I would be safe if I did.

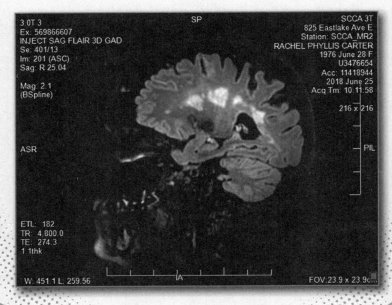

3.0T 3
Ex: 569866607
INJECT SAG FLAIR 3D GAD
Se: 401/13
Im: 201 (ASC)
Sag: R 25.04

Mag: 2.1
(BSpline)

ASR

SP

SCCA 3T
825 Eastlake Ave E
Station: SCCA_MR2
RACHEL PHYLLIS CARTER
1976 June 28 F
U3476654
Acc: 11418944
2018 June 25
Acq Tm: 10:11:58

216 x 216

PIL

ETL: 182
TR: 4,800.0
TE: 274.3
1.1thk

W: 451.1 L: 259.56

IA

FOV:23.9 x 23.9c...

5

IMAGINARY BRANCHES
AND REAL HOLES

Losing my ability to run and then, slowly, my ability to do many normal daily functions was incredibly hard and heartbreaking. But the next period of my life almost destroyed me. This is not an easy time for me to remember or to talk about. But this period, when I became unrecognizable to myself, is one of the central points of my story. I could no longer set goals, focus my thoughts, or make simple choices. I just did what was essential to get through each moment. And then the next moment. And at some point, I wasn't sure that I wanted there to be any more next moments.

Two obstacles I faced at this time felt crushingly insurmountable. One was work, and the other was pain.

I loved my job, and I was good at it. My boss, Dennis, appreciated my sales skills and my understanding of the lumber industry. I developed many strong relationships there, both with customers and coworkers. I felt valued and needed.

This was actually my second time with this company. I had left the same position to have my third child, Hannah, and had started graduate school three days after she was born. But the bills were piling up, and Josh and I faced the reality that I needed to go back to work. I now realize how crazy this all was, trying to start a new career while having a newborn at home. But these were the days when I was still trying to make more out of my life, before the disability really hit me.

After I returned to work everything went smoothly for a while, but my symptoms were becoming increasingly noticeable. I started to panic; I did not want anyone to pity me, and I did not want MS to define my identity. I couldn't imagine quitting my job, but the devastating truth was I could no longer hide my condition.

I had been with the company for eight years. A handful of people knew I had MS, but it was not common knowledge. I never brought it up, and—to the best of my knowledge—upper management did not know. So when I started missing work often I decided it was time to open up. I just wasn't sure how. I didn't want to make a big announcement about it, as I had done when I shared the news of my pregnancies.

I decided to do it slowly and without drama. Through individual conversations, I explained my situation to all my coworkers. I even made sure my customers knew why I was missing work and reassured them that the sales staff was up to date on their accounts.

Revealing my condition at work had benefits and drawbacks. My receptionist started holding calls when I was clearly in so much pain that she didn't think I could speak to customers. She often saw me in tears. My coworkers were all uncomfortable from simply not knowing what to do. I fell down, I bumped into desks, I could hardly write—and they all just ignored it. I would get angry when they ignored my falls, but I also didn't know what I wanted them *to* do. They were all doing their best to make me feel comfortable and deflect attention from the fact that I was clearly suffering. I could not have expected any more from them.

Eventually I came to realize that being open about my disease was a good thing. When I jokingly mentioned that I might be ready for a walker, someone from the office pulled me aside. He told me that he had a very nice walker sitting in his shed not being used. He had purchased it for his father right before he passed. When he offered it to me I reluctantly agreed to give it a try. When he brought it in the next day, I decided I wanted to personalize it. How could I make a navy blue walker purchased for a ninety-year-old man look like something the fashionable, thirty-seven-year-old me would feel comfortable with? I went to a craft store. I bought stickers and rhinestones, and asked my coworkers to help me bling it out.

After several particularly difficult and disruptive months, Dennis asked me if I wanted to stop working and go on disability. As my boss, he was not legally allowed to ask me this, but he was not asking as my boss; he was asking as my friend. He was a very kind man, and was always very fatherly toward me. His son had cystic fibrosis and had almost died before he got a lung transplant, so he had empathy for my situation. He made every allowance he could for me, and I was grateful. Most companies would have let me go by now.

But I was not ready to hear the word *disability*. As crazy as it sounds, I was still truly shocked at the end of the day when I was so tired I couldn't walk to my car by myself—even though it happened every day. No wonder people were beginning to question my judgment about continuing to work. Albert Einstein is popularly credited with defining insanity as "doing the same thing over and over and expecting a different result." I was living the definition at that point.

I was so miserable at the end of every workday that, on my way home, I frequently imagined driving off the road into the river. There was no end to my misery; this was my life now. Fortunately I always remembered I had three kids depending on me to come home. When I got there, I would walk through my front door and collapse on the floor crying. My poor kids would not know what to do. They would just huddle around me on the floor, hugging me and telling me they were making me better. I had told them that what they could do for me was to give me love, and in a way their actions did make me feel better. At least *they* didn't feel so helpless in those moments.

The other obstacle making life unbearable at this point was pain. It was mind-numbing neuropathic pain that was impossible to ignore. It consumed me. And it changed me. It was overwhelming, and it shut down my brain.

There were two types of neuropathic pain that I had already started experiencing sporadically. One was a deep continuous ache in my arms, which I referred to as "hollow bones." The second I called "the irritants"; a sensation like bugs crawling under my skin. When I got these from time to time it was bearable, but when they started to plague me daily it was maddening. Yet hollow bones and the irritants weren't the worst of it.

I was at work when a new type of neuropathic pain hit me. I was sitting at my desk when out of nowhere I felt a burning sensation on my back. I asked my good friend Erica to go into the restroom with me and take a look. It felt as if I had a sunburn or a severe rash. Erica said she saw nothing, and I tried to fathom what could be happening. How could she see nothing when it hurt so badly? It didn't take me long to realize it must be MS related. There was no other explanation. Over the next week or two, the pain got worse and worse until it no longer felt like a sunburn. It now felt as if someone had poured a vat of boiling oil onto my back. I was desperate for relief, but because it was not "real" pain, regular pain pills would not do anything to lessen it. There was no inflammation to reduce; it was just my nerves screaming at the top of their lungs. I now had "phantom burns."

The only thing that dulled these sensations was a serious narcotic. I began to pop several pills every four hours just to be able to function minimally. My general practitioner gave me a prescription for Vicodin. When I was taking three or four Vicodin at a time and was still in severe pain, he suggested I switch to Fentanyl. Fentanyl is delivered through a patch on the arm; the drug released itself slowly through my skin.

The first day was amazing. I put the patch on in the evening right after we picked up the prescription; the next day I woke up with no pain for the first time in months. I actually went to the gym! I thought my life was going to return to normal and I could be me again. I was high all day—not from the narcotic, but from the absence of pain. I went to bed feeling more than happy. I was elated to finally have relief, and hopefully a permanent solution.

In the middle of the night I woke up and looked around feeling very confused. I had no idea where I was. I lifted my head from the bed to look out of the bedroom window, and I saw a parking lot with a tree in it. This did not make any sense to me because we had a backyard, not a paved parking lot, behind our house, and there certainly was no tree near the window. The next thing I knew, the branches of the tree were visibly growing—through our *closed* window and into the bedroom. I woke Josh and asked him where we were. I thought we must be in a hotel or some other unfamiliar location. He calmly reassured me everything was okay; I was at home in bed. I drifted back to sleep, dismissing this hallucination as a strangely realistic dream.

Around 6 a.m. I woke up with one of the worst migraines I have ever experienced. I hadn't had a migraine in years. I had stopped having them when I got pregnant, so this reoccurrence was unusual and distressing. Josh was so alarmed at the severity of it that he stayed home from work. He didn't want to leave me alone even for the twenty minutes it would take to get the kids to school, so they stayed home too.

After taking four Advil, I finally was able to fall back to sleep. Around 10 a.m. I woke up again. My head didn't hurt quite as much, but now I was delusional and completely disoriented. Had I had gone completely insane? I went downstairs desperate to find Josh. I knelt down on the floor in a yoga "child's pose" and started slapping the floor with my hands to get his attention. Miraculously, I was able to make a connection between the nightmare I was experiencing and the Fentanyl patch on my arm. I knew it was causing this madness—but that was literally all I knew. I started wailing like a deranged person. In between sobs and screams I begged Josh to take the patch off.

Josh was on the phone at this point, frantically trying to get advice. He was afraid that taking the patch off incorrectly could cause the pouch to burst and release all the drug into my skin at once. He knew he had to talk to a doctor or risk overdosing me. With all of the chaos, it was a miracle he was able to remain calm enough to get someone on the phone. Remembering how loudly I was howling, I'm amazed our neighbors didn't call the police. I can't imagine what our children were thinking, and I never want to know.

Josh finally got word that he could remove the patch gently without any danger, and he did. I spent the rest of the day in bed with massive amounts of sweat pouring off me. I must have changed my sleep clothes half a dozen times. It was disgusting. I slept off and on throughout that day and night—and woke in pain again. So the cycle of figuring out how to survive my hollow bones, irritants, and phantom burns started all over again.

I went back to my general practitioner; this time he put me on Oxycodone. He said it was quicker and longer-lasting than Vicodin. I could take four pills at a time, four times a day. But no more; that was the maximum. He told me very gently, "I don't want to sound cold, but my goal is not for you to live without any pain. That will probably never be possible for you. I am just trying to make the pain bearable." I burst into tears.

I really did try to stick to the four-pill dosage, but the burning got so bad at times that I would have to take six pills to get any relief.

ⓔ·ⓔ·ⓔ

Soon after the Fentanyl crisis, my neurologist— I'll call him Dr. S —told me he could no longer help me. Dr. S had been my neurologist for eight years. When I picture him now I see a middle-aged man who looks like the stereotype of a mad scientist. Dr. S had been recommended to me by someone I met in an MS support group when I was first diagnosed.

Because of how I had learned about Dr. S, I had always assumed he was an MS specialist, but I was wrong. He was a neurologist who specialized in strokes, not MS. He also didn't have the greatest bedside manner. He never looked at me when we talked, he always had his eyes on the computer, and he never seemed to remember anything about me or my case. But I thought he was smart, and I had it in my head that he was an MS specialist, so I trusted his care. Learning he was not an MS specialist was a real blow. Even though leaving his practice was for the best—and I clearly *needed* an MS specialist—being abandoned by my doctor was disheartening. If he thought I was too far gone for him to treat, I must be hopeless. His last act as my neurologist was to prescribe a new DMT called Gilenya. At least this new drug was a pill, not an injection.

Dr. S recommended I go to Oregon Health and Science University (OHSU), a top research hospital. When I had my first MRI at OHSU, the neurologist working that day was Dr. A. She was a petite Indian woman with a lilting accent. She seemed more competent and more informed on MS than any doctor I had sought treatment from so far. On top of that, she was kind and sensitive to my fragile mental state. I was confident I was in good hands.

After analyzing my first MRI since transferring to OHSU, Dr. A discovered I had developed over twenty new lesions since my previous MRI. This made a total of at least fifty-five lesions, and three black holes. Looking at my MRI with Dr. A, I felt as if we were looking at a horrifying science experiment. I could not wrap my (apparently hole-filled) brain around the fact that *this* was the organ responsible for my thinking. As I stared at the black-and-white image of my brain, it seemed like a miracle I was able to think at all. At the end of the appointment Dr. A suggested I try a new DMT that reportedly was more effective than Gilenya: Tysabri. Although Tysabri could be taken only for two years, she was confident that newer and better drugs would come out before two years had passed.

I projected my frustration onto Dr. S. How could he have let this happen to me? I had been a model patient. I had told him every time I felt a twinge or a tingle. In retrospect, I think part of the reason he missed so much was that I was constantly working out to stay strong. I can still hear his voice saying, "You're not weak enough to be having a relapse." He said it time after time. But *I* could tell when I was having a relapse. My brain would always get very foggy, and I would experience a new symptom, or worsening of old symptoms, like loss of balance. In retrospect, I should have trusted myself more.

But I had many other things to worry about at this point. I couldn't work effectively. I was in constant pain.

Giant pieces of my brain had disappeared. And now I was on a new and dangerous DMT with very scary side effects—including death.

I wasn't losing just my quality of life. I was losing my life.

6

STEPPING INTO THIN AIR

In 2013, before things got really rough during Hybrid, Josh and I had decided to enroll our two older children, Marin and Noah, in a private Christian school that was close to my office. This allowed me to drop them off on my way to work and pick them up on the way home. I mention this because, like many other twists in my story, this seemingly insignificant decision changed the course of my life.

The new school worked out well until my MS symptoms worsened. Often I left work early and had to pick the kids up before school was over. Because I was picking them up earlier and earlier, I felt I had to tell the school staff about my situation. They were understanding and accommodating. Marin's teacher told me that she wanted me to meet one of the other moms. Her name was Suzie, and she also had MS.

I met other people with MS all the time. Usually we swapped stories and talked symptoms; this is what I expected would happen when I met Suzie. I always enjoyed expanding my MS network, but Suzie was about to blow up my world.

Some days I would make it through the entire day of work, and it was on one of these days that I eventually met Suzie. We were both in the parking lot loading up kids. I introduced myself and explained that I had MS and had been told that she did as well. Looking at her, I saw a healthy, pretty, energetic young mom. I caught myself thinking that she looked just fine. I stopped myself immediately, because, as I knew firsthand, MS is a largely invisible disease. I had no way of knowing what stage of the disease she was living in. She couldn't see my pain, and I couldn't see hers. "How long have you had MS?" I asked.

"Three years," she replied, "but I am ready for this nightmare to be over." As I stood there clutching my car door for support, I thought, *Three years is nothing, bitch. Wait till you're where I am.* But I kept my mouth in check and gave no response. She continued, "I'm trying to get into Dr. Burt's study in Chicago."

Dr. Burt? She mentioned the study as if I should know all about it. I had to consciously keep my mouth from dropping open. "What study?" I asked, trying to sound casual and knowing I was failing. Then Suzie said five words that meant nothing to my comprehension but everything to a hope it suddenly stirred: autologous hematopoietic stem cell transplantation, or HSCT.

"The study involves a treatment that cures MS," Suzie said.

"You must be mistaken," I responded. "There's no cure for MS."

"Yes there is, and it's happening in Chicago," she insisted. "There's a Facebook group for HSCT patients. I'll invite you to join it when I get home. It has a lot of information."

"Thank you," I said lightly, giving her a friendly smile as I got into my car. I wanted her to think I believed her, but I could tell I wasn't pulling it off. I had heard about so many false cures in the past; it did not seem possible that there was an *actual* cure for MS and that I had no knowledge of it. But as I drove, I couldn't get the conversation out of mind. Could there really be a cure? I wanted to get on that Facebook page as soon as I could. Even if it wasn't a cure, Suzie was talking about a legitimate medical study being done, right here in the United States. *Maybe...?* I ignored the speed limit on my way home.

I can't explain exactly what shifted in me after meeting Suzie, but I was different. In the months prior to learning about HSCT my emotional life had primarily consisted of psyching myself up to carry out the most basic tasks and trying not to cry. Now, suddenly, I had something to focus on other than just surviving. No other real options for improving my health had ever been presented to me—nothing except trying the latest drug while continuing to decline. I became fixated on HSCT.

Josh felt the shift too; immediately after hearing about my conversation with Suzie he began researching HSCT.

What neither of us could understand was how a treatment for this incurable disease could exist when not one of my doctors had ever mentioned it. After all, I was being treated at one of the best research hospitals in the country. Both Josh and my father were keen and relentless researchers. They were determined to keep up with every new development in treating MS. How had none of us heard of this?

This wasn't the first time we had looked into options outside the medical mainstream. The summer before, I had met another mother in our circle who worked for a company that specialized in sending people overseas for medical treatments that were unaffordable in the United States. She had tried to talk me into going to Mexico for a treatment that uses balloons to enlarge the veins leading into the brain. Ultimately, we could find no evidence that this treatment was valid: the rate at which blood enters the brain has nothing to do with the size of the veins, and blood flow has nothing to do with MS. What I was learning was that there are many snake oil salesmen out there taking advantage of people in desperate circumstances.

It also seemed as if *everyone* had a suggestion about my health and how to improve it. Many of the suggestions involved dietary restrictions that were just too hard to live with. I did stick to a gluten-free diet for several years and I think it did make me feel better. I had no idea, however, whether I felt better because of the diet or because it was one small thing I could control in my life. Nothing I tried ever stopped or slowed the progression of my disease.

HSCT felt different. Even though the only information available online was from word-of-mouth sources like blogs and Facebook pages, the reported results coming out of countries like Italy and Russia were nothing short of miraculous. The people posting these reports had all been involved in medical trials like the one in Chicago that Suzie had told me about.

The theory behind using HSCT as a treatment for RRMS is pretty simple. If the malfunctioning immune system is destroyed by a high dose of chemotherapy and regenerated using stem cells from the same individual, the immune system is essentially "reset." In the patients we read about online, this resetting process prevented further attacks on the nerves and the myelin, halting the neurological damage and allowing the body to recover some or all of the ability that had been lost during previous exacerbations.

HSCT is a common treatment for several types of cancer. It is essentially the same as a bone marrow transplant. As a treatment for MS, it was considered experimental at this time because the results of the trials had yet to be published in medical journals. But HSCT was reported to halt disease progression in RRMS patients in over 85 percent of cases, and the mortality rate was about 4 percent.

After all the despair, helplessness, and fear of the previous three years, reading about such promising results was overwhelming. Josh and I were reeling with emotion. We weren't used to good news. We knew we had to tell my parents about it immediately. We weren't seeking their advice; the decision to pursue HSCT had been made. But we knew we would need their support to get through it.

HSCT treatment requires patients to spend weeks or months in the hospital. It takes another five years to recover and rebuild the immune system. This was not something our nuclear family could pursue alone; we had to get a support team on board. Clearly I would be out of commission for an extended period of time, and Josh had to continue to work. We needed people to help care for our children, and I would need a caretaker to help me navigate the logistics surrounding my treatment.

We were fortunate that my parents were retired and in good health. They were also dedicated family people, always staying connected with their kids and grandkids. Even though they lived three hours away, there were many occasions when one or both of them would hop in the car and show up to help out when I was overcome with MS-related problems.

When we approached my parents with the information about this unknown and risky treatment, they were understandably taken aback. These were the same lovely people who had patiently listened to and supported me through numerous wild schemes and life-changing plans during my young adulthood. They knew the stakes were very high at this point, and they were worried to death. They also suspected that HSCT was too good to be true. I was not surprised by this; it was the same reaction Josh and I had both had initially. But within a day of our conversation, my parents called back. They told me how nuts I had sounded at first, but—after doing their own research—they were all in.

The next step was telling Dr. I, my GP, about my intention to pursue this unorthodox treatment. The conversation did not go well. He had known me and my family for years. He had delivered two of my children and supported me through years of struggles with MS. He had worked hard to alleviate my neuropathic pain. It was disheartening when his first reaction was resoundingly negative. I was caught off guard. He was immediately against pursuing HSCT. He felt it was too risky. He told me, "You really don't know what you're getting into." I was touched that he seemed so concerned for my safety, but I told him I was not asking him; I was informing him of my plans. I was just hoping he would support me in my recovery afterward. He was still apprehensive and wanted to find out more about the procedure. He reluctantly said, "If you go forward with this, I will see you through the recovery. Just make sure all of the related paperwork and reports are sent to me."

The next person I wanted to get on board was my neurologist, Dr. A. Surprisingly, even she had never heard of a stem cell transplant being used for MS. To her credit, she listened to me. She turned to her computer, and it took her only a few minutes to be convinced that this was a credible study. She even started talking about doing her own study at OHSU. But we agreed I could not afford the time it would take for her to fund and establish a longitudinal medical trial; that could take years. And the longer I waited for treatment the more disabled I would become.

⊙•⊙•⊙

With the limited information we had, Josh and I began investigating the clinical trial we'd heard about: Dr. Richard Burt's study at Northwestern University in Chicago. Dr. Burt was the chief of immunotherapy and autoimmune diseases there, a high credential. Josh ferreted out the appropriate contact information and requested the paperwork. We filled it out, then waited anxiously. A few weeks later, a nurse called and said that based on the information we had submitted I was a possible candidate for their study—but there was a two-month wait even to be evaluated. Josh asked her to contact us if there was a cancellation, and the following week she called! We were elated and immediately scheduled a trip to Chicago. It was shocking that a slot had opened up that quickly. Yet another sign; this was meant to be.

Josh and I made plans for our trip to Chicago. Travel had always been part of our life together, and I had never been to Chicago. As a treat to ourselves, we decided to fly in a few days ahead of the medical appointments. I was not particularly excited about sightseeing; I wasn't even sure I would have the strength to leave the hotel. But, perhaps because I was full of hope, I had a rush of energy, and we were able to get out and see a bit of Chicago after all.

On our second day there we went to the Willis Tower (formerly the Sears Tower). At 110 stories, it is one of the tallest buildings in the world, and the tallest building in the United States. When we got to the top of this skyscraper, I mustered up my courage and stepped out onto the glass floor of the famous Skydeck. Seeing the ground more than 1,300 feet beneath me was amazing and terrifying. I knew it was safe, but something about stepping out onto what looks like thin air was a heavy reminder of my mortality and how close I felt to the end of my life. I was more than a thousand feet above the ground with nothing visible holding me up. It took my breath away.

On the way back to the hotel, we experienced one of Chicago's famous downpours. The rain came so fast and so hard it was as if someone had flipped the switch on an instant storm machine. As we stood under an awning waiting for the deluge to stop, I watched the droplets beat down and thought about how quickly my illness had taken over my life. When the storm disappeared as suddenly as it had begun, I said a quick prayer that my MS would end in the same abrupt way.

The next day was my first appointment. The assessment team had scheduled an MRI for me, but I didn't need to be there until three o'clock. I was pretty exhausted, so our big-city excursion for the day was simply going to a restaurant to try authentic Chicago-style pizza (which I failed to appreciate). After that we headed to the hospital.

I was scared. In fact, I felt a complete panic coming on. The results of the MRI would determine whether or not Dr. Burt would accept me into the study. The thought that I might be rejected nauseated me. Walking the block to the hospital felt like walking to my doom. It was a very long, dark block. It wasn't the procedure I feared; all I had to do was get an MRI that would take a longer than usual. I had had a million MRIs before, but none of them had felt this important. I wanted to throw up.

When it was all over and I got back to the hotel, I collapsed. The emotional strain of the day as well as the usual pain and fatigue were almost too much to bear, but I still held on to a glimmer of the excitement that had powered me this far. My father had arrived that day, and he would be with us for tomorrow's consultations. We would all meet with the neurologist and the internist heading up the study. I fell asleep thinking about how long I had waited for the possibility of some good news or definite answers.

The following morning, we met with the neurologist, Dr. O. He led me through a series of tests I had done many times before: walking heel to toe, standing with my eyes closed until I fell over, walking on my tiptoes.

Then Dr. O gave me a test that was new to me. He asked me to walk on my heels. It was the weirdest thing—I could not do it at all, not even for one step. I was telling my body to perform the action, yet nothing happened. The connections to do this task weren't there anymore. Great! One more thing I could no longer do. I collapsed in tears.

The doctor stepped out of the office, politely telling me he would give me a moment while he went to check on the results of the MRI. Josh and my father put their arms around me and I felt better—but only briefly. After I had pulled myself together, Dr. O came back with bad news. He didn't think I was an ideal patient for their study. I was right on the cusp of meeting the requirements; the decision was in the hands of Dr. Burt.

At this moment, something inside me clicked into action. From out of nowhere, the badass Rachel I hadn't seen in years awoke and took over the conversation. I made and maintained eye contact with Dr. O and began my argument. "I know HSCT is a tough thing to go through. If you're looking for people who can get through this treatment successfully, I am your ideal candidate. I have been through more difficult situations than you know. I am tough as nails, and when I set my mind to something, I don't back down. I can get through anything. I will certainly be a success in your study. I can do this. If anyone will have positive results, it's me." Dr. O looked at me for a long moment. He appeared touched by my determination, even though we both knew that being mentally tough was not a criterion for being accepted into the study. He was going to try to persuade Dr. Burt to put me in the trial.

Next we were called in by Kimberly, the assisting nurse, to meet Dr. Burt. After months of assigning so much importance to his name, it didn't surprise me that his presence filled the room. It was not only his considerable size and commanding voice that dominated; it was his air of confidence. He skipped the small talk and immediately asked me to tell him my history, cutting me off frequently to ask clarifying questions. He was very brusque and appeared to be in a hurry. We only talked for only a few minutes before he said, "I'm just going to be honest with you. You are not an ideal candidate for my study. But I will not say no yet. I will get back to you with an answer." And he left the room.

I looked at Kimberly in disbelief. "But he didn't write any notes!" I sputtered. "He barely got any information! How does he know anything about me?"

"Don't worry. That's what I'm for," Kimberly answered with a knowing chuckle. "I'll make sure he gets all the information. He'll look over your medical history and your MRIs and talk to Dr. O. After that, he will make a decision."

"But I need to have this treatment . . ." I choked, trying to keep from dissolving into tears.

"I know how you must feel," Kimberly assured me. "The main reason Dr. Burt is hesitating to accept you into the study is that your MRI showed no recent exacerbations. Perhaps you've moved into secondary-progressive, and this study is only for relapsing-remitting. If you stop taking your current DMT, you might have a flare-up and be accepted." I followed her advice and stopped taking Tysabri. I learned later that doing this was a mistake.

After being reassured by Kimberly that we would hear something within a week, Josh, my father, and I left the hospital feeling a little more hopeful. At least we would have an answer soon. Our flight home was only a couple hours away and our bags were already packed, so we got a cab directly to the airport. Once we arrived, I remembered the long flight of stairs I had taken note of when we flew in. I dreaded the climb. The excitement and buzz of pursuing treatment at Northwestern was completely spent. I just wanted to be home in my bed, not fighting with stairs. I needed no more reminders of how sick I was.

While Josh carried my bag, I gathered my resolve and took the first step. Three steps later I felt as if I had climbed a hundred. But I kept going. I knew I had to get to the top. I just kept taking one more step. My steps got slower and slower, but I didn't stop. Once I made it to the top, I dropped to the ground.

The airport agent stationed there looked alarmed and asked if I was all right. My father casually said, "Yes, this is just what happens. She'll be fine." He knew I didn't like it when people pitied me. He and Josh stood nearby, reassuring people I was okay. I sat there for several minutes until I felt I could walk to the gate. Josh asked if I wanted a wheelchair. "No!" I snapped. "I can walk to the fucking gate!" I wasn't mad at him; I was just overwhelmed with exhaustion and frustration. Luckily, Josh understood exactly where my testiness was directed. He was just as invested as I was in this trip. Together, we walked slowly toward the gate to catch our flight home.

When it was almost time to board, my phone rang. "Hi Rachel, it's Kimberly, from the hospital. I wanted to catch you before you got on the plane. You got into the trial!"

I couldn't believe it. Dr. Burt had been so negative and the interaction had been so brief; I had thought for sure I wasn't getting in. I was so elated that I actually felt dizzy. Josh and my dad were practically jumping up and down in their molded plastic seats.

"I wish we had time to get a martini!" I told my father. That was our drink. We always drank one when we were together celebrating something. Then, right on cue, a message came over the loudspeaker: "Flight 781 to Portland has been delayed. It will be boarding in three hours."

We all laughed and headed to the nearest airport bar to celebrate.

ᕮ·ᕮ·ᕮ

Two days after we got home, I received a second call from Kimberly. This time it was not good news. "I'm so sorry," she said. "I made a mistake. You are not in the trial. Your MRI showed no new or active lesions. Dr. Burt suspects your disease may have moved into secondary-progressive MS. We will reevaluate your case in one year."

I thanked Kimberly robotically and hung up the phone with her voice echoing in my head: *I made a mistake. Secondary-progressive. One year.*

"I don't have a year," I said aloud to the empty room. I let the truth hang there in the silence for a moment, then slowly stood and went to find Josh.

7

THE FIGHT BEFORE
THE FIGHT

Losing the opportunity to get into the Chicago trial was an enormous blow. I had built up my hopes for recovering my life with this treatment. I was convinced that all the signs were pointing to Chicago and that it was going to happen. I was now completely deflated. I was more than heartbroken; I was broken. I didn't know how I could face my reality anymore. Josh held me while I cried myself to sleep that night. "We are not giving up. We will get you in somewhere else," he assured me as I wept.

It was amazing to me how quickly the rest of my "team" bounced back. It was clear that Josh and my parents were as fully committed to pursuing this treatment as I was. Giving up was not an option. Shortly after the Chicago letdown, my father called to tell me that he had sent out inquiries to hospitals in Italy, Germany, and Russia that were using HSCT to treat MS patients. If those places didn't respond, there were other less familiar options like India, Mexico, and Israel.

Out of all the possibilities, our goal was still the United States. The only other place we were aware of that was doing a study similar to the one at Northwestern was the Seattle Cancer Care Alliance (SCCA) in Washington State, just three hours from home. The SCCA was in partnership with the Fred Hutchinson Cancer Research Center and the University of Washington. Dr. George Georges was the medical oncologist at "The Hutch" and was doing a phase II trial in conjunction with both Dr. James Bowen, a neurologist specializing in MS at the Swedish Medical Center, and the University of Washington hospital.

While investigating alternatives, we found that Chicago and Seattle were performing HSCT using slightly different approaches: myeloablative and non-myeloablative. In myeloablative HSCT, the patient's immune system is almost completely destroyed by removing the damaging types of white blood cells as well as the bone marrow. In non-myeloablative HSCT, the immune system is only diminished. This protocol has a much quicker recovery time, but also a lower success rate. Seattle offered myeloablative HSCT. As we discussed and thought about the two protocols, our team all favored getting rid of every one of those damn cells that were killing me!

No matter where I ended up, in Seattle or abroad, it was now painfully obvious that we had to make plans for our children. The humiliating fact was that I was no longer an active parent and would soon be living away from our home for weeks, if not months. Josh and I talked about it for a long time and in the end we decided we had to find temporary homes for our three children. Fortunately, we had generous offers from family members. With Christmas and winter break approaching, it seemed best to have Marin (third grade) and Noah (kindergarten) begin their new schools in their new homes with our relatives after the holidays. After many phone calls and much deliberation, we placed Marin with Josh's sister's family on the Oregon coast. She fit in nicely with two cousins near her age and a baby girl cousin as well. Noah and Hannah would go to my parents' house. We needed Josh to be able to continue working with fewer pressures at home.

☯·☯·☯

My father had started talking regularly with Bernie McLaughlin, the study coordinator in Seattle. Dr. Georges was incredibly encouraging—the opposite of what we had experienced in Chicago. The team in Seattle had seen my records and saw no reason why I shouldn't be in the study. Bernie told us that I was in as long as I passed the necessary tests and could fund it. We were, once again, ecstatic.

Within a few weeks I was in Seattle preparing to start a four-day regimen of tests that would determine if I was healthy enough to endure a stem cell transplant. My father accompanied me, and we found a hotel near the hospital.

The idea was that we could walk there if I felt up to it. The hospital was at the top of a steep hill. Although it put me out of breath, I made the three-block climb and felt proud of myself.

When we arrived at SCCA we went to the registration area, where they were expecting me. After I filled out paperwork, a nurse's assistant guided us to a room where I would wait with many other patients for a blood draw. Finally we took the elevator to the fifth floor, where I would meet my medical team. I was anxious as we stepped through the sliding doors.

"Rachel, Mike, it is so nice to finally meet you face-to-face," Bernie said warmly as if she had known us for years. Then she laughed and said, "Rachel, I was questioning that you existed, since all my conversations have been with Josh and your father."

I laughed too. "Honestly, Bernie, I have not been functioning well and couldn't trust myself to have a serious phone conversation. But I heard all about you from Dad and Josh. This is just one more symptom for you to put in my records—my brain is fried!" Bernie's incredible friendliness and confidence were contagious. This tall energetic woman had convinced me in less than five minutes that I was right where I belonged.

After introducing us to the receptionist, Bernie suggested sitting in the waiting room while we went over the plan for the day. "You'll be spending a lot of time here," she said. The room was set up for comfort. We sat in gray recliners and looked out on a panoramic view of the harbor. As she went over the schedule we saw a seaplane taking off from the bay, something that caught my dad's eye. I wondered how many seaplanes we might see over the next few months.

After an X-ray of my lungs and an EKG, I met Dr. Georges, the head of the study. I had envisioned this person as a godlike being. After all, he was making history, and he was going to save my life. But Dr. Georges turned out to be a thin man who wore glasses atop his beak-like nose. He spoke slowly and didn't always make eye contact. It didn't take me long to realize that this was because he wanted to make sure he explained everything thoroughly. Every word was carefully considered so that he knew I clearly understood him. He was thoughtful and highly intelligent. Even though I had only just met him, I was ready to put my future in his hands.

"This is going to be very hard on you," Dr. Georges said. "I need to make sure you understand that this is a risky procedure. There is a small but significant chance that you could die. You may change your mind at any point before you begin the HSCT." Although he said this very calmly, I felt a heaviness fall over the room. But I thought about it only for a millisecond.

"Dr. Georges, we have put in a lot of effort to be here, and in my current state of health, I do not feel that I have a choice. I am definitely ready to do this no matter how hard or risky it is," I replied.

"I thought so," he said with the first smile I had seen from him.

It was obvious to me that he actually cared about me as a person and not just as a study subject. "Can I hug you?" I said. Dr. Georges hesitated, then awkwardly opened his arms.

My first meeting with Dr. Georges gave me a lot of confidence in him, but it wasn't all good news. When we reviewed my history, I told him that the staff in Chicago had encouraged me to stop taking Tysabri, the DMT I had been on at the time. Dr. Georges looked at me for a few seconds when I shared that detail. "Why would they tell you to do that?" he asked finally. It was an uncomfortable moment; he obviously disagreed strongly with this recommendation. I answered as best I could: Dr. Burt wouldn't consider treating me with Tysabri in my system. Dr. Georges, on the other hand, saw no reason why treatment couldn't begin while I was on it. I might have avoided the exacerbation I had had after my visit to Chicago if I had kept taking that medication.

The next key person we met was Dr. Bowen. As head neurologist, he was equally important to the study. His office was across town. We drove there the following day after getting my one-millionth MRI at SCCA. Dr. Bowen was a talker. Between checking my hand strength and watching me walk down the hall, he chatted and told us stories. While observing that I couldn't walk more than fifty feet without putting a steadying hand on a wall, he told me the history of various pieces of medical equipment.

Every patient at SCCA was assigned to a team, and each team had a color. On the last day of testing, I got to meet my team, the Gold Team. Patients' information packets were put into folders that matched the teams' colors. As a patient of the Gold Team, I was looking forward to a glittery golden envelope with my name on it. Instead I was handed a manila folder. I was not happy about this. If I was going to have a folder, it was not going to be generic!

When I met the nurses, the folder was the first thing I brought up, with a smile on my face so that they knew I was half joking. They would be assigned to my care for the length of my stay as an outpatient. If they were going to be in charge of me from beginning to end, I figured they should know my personality right away. All three of them passed my test, laughing at my joke. "You can decorate your file yourself before you check in for treatment if that would make you feel better," one of them said. I was relieved they had a sense of humor. We would need it to get through the coming weeks.

Before leaving Seattle, I was told that SCCA had accepted me into their study. This team had over forty years of stem cell transplants under their belt. They were the most experienced, and they wanted me! I might not have been able to walk fifty feet, but I was walking on cloud nine.

☺•☺•☺

In our early contact with SCCA, we had been told I would be accepted into their study if I could pass the physical test and if I could fund the treatment. Our insurance through Josh's work had covered each pretreatment test, so we assumed it would also cover the HSCT. This turned out not to be the case. The insurance company swiftly rejected my request for coverage, and I fell off cloud nine.

We immediately appealed, and the insurance company denied the appeal just as swiftly. The unexpected rejection felt like a punch in the gut. Why would they meet the cost of the massive amounts of pretesting if they had no intention of covering the procedure?

Since the trip to Chicago, I could not get it out of my mind that I might have moved into secondary-progressive MS. The race for HSCT was on. Most research showed that HSCT has a much lower success rate with SPMS patients, and many programs will not accept someone who has advanced to this stage. In my case, with my current rate of decline, not getting into an HSCT program would mean the pain would never stop and I would be in a wheelchair full time by the end of the year.

The cost of treatment in Seattle made it almost impossible to consider paying for it out of pocket. My family is lucky enough to be financially stable, but there was no way we could come up with the $500,000 needed. (The cost of the Chicago study was $150,000, which was still a lot of money but within the realm of possibility.) The only options for getting treatment in Seattle were, one, to offer the hospital cash and see if they would lower the price or, two, to convince our insurance company to cover me.

My father started looking into other options, one at a hospital in Heidelberg, Germany, and another in Florence,

Italy, but we hadn't given up the possibility of Seattle. We decided to hire an attorney, Ms. G., to advise us on how to make the strongest case possible in our second appeal for coverage. We figured getting correspondence on legal letterhead would get the attention of the insurance company and let them know we were not giving up easily. This was now a war against Big Insurance.

The emails flew like a flock of worried birds between my dad, Josh, Bernie, Dr. Georges, and Ms. G. Between October 2013 and January 2014, the five of them exchanged 112 messages.

Ms. G. felt that the key to a successful appeal was to show "clear medical evidence" that the treatment would be effective in improving my condition. My father reached out to Dr. Georges for his input on how to make it clear that HSCT was not "experimental." It is a common treatment for cancer and had been used recently—with success—all over the world to treat MS. Josh also researched a list of insurance company approvals for HSCT (and found that there were not many) in the hopes that precedents would strengthen our case.

Josh and my father also figured out how much money my current ineffective treatments were costing the insurance company. If HSCT worked, it would save them a *lot* of money. That year alone, I had already run up $121,000 in medical expenses, and it was only October. My bills in the years prior had averaged about $51,000 per year. If my decline was to continue, which seemed likely, the bills would get bigger every year.

While my family was crunching numbers and doing research, Ms. G. was corresponding with Dr. Georges about the appeal letter. Dr. Georges answered questions about the medical necessity of the treatment, the efficiency and cost-effectiveness with which it would be administered, peer-reviewed evidence of safety, and how the treatment was clinically appropriate and consistent with my diagnosis. Ms. G. was very thorough and completely satisfied that Dr. Georges' answers not only met the criteria put forth by the insurance company but also addressed all the reasons they had given for my initial denial.

But the insurance company did not agree with Ms. G. or Dr. Georges.

By the final conference call with Ms. G. on Christmas Eve 2013, our war with the insurance company came to an end. The last appeal to the external review board was denied. After a few more emails with Ms. G., our flock of worried birds fell to the ground with a thud.

☙ • ☙ • ☙

We were back to square one. Again. Almost without skipping a beat though, my father reached out to the doctor in Italy with whom he had been communicating, knowing we might need a backup plan. He and Dr. Saccardi began discussing what would need to happen for us to schedule treatment at Careggi University Hospital in Florence.

Although we hated the idea of separating our family further, our options were limited. The out-of-pocket cost for Seattle was untenable. My dad had attempted to negotiate with the hospital, but they would not take less for a cash payment. Josh had looked into fundraising and had started a HopeHelpLive website that our friends and family could donate to, but it seemed highly unlikely that we could raise half a million dollars. Italy began to feel like our only choice.

But it wasn't just the distance between Oregon and Italy that was bothering Josh. Something about the denial of our appeals didn't sit right with him. He couldn't get past the fact that the insurance company had approved the testing I needed to get *into* the clinical trial, but not the trial itself. He decided to talk to his employer directly.

Josh worked for a huge multinational corporation with a self-funded health plan. This means his company has a lot of influence in coverage decisions. The insurance company only administers the plan; the employer pays all of the claims. This also meant it was extremely confusing to figure out whom to approach to talk to about our circumstances.

He started with the leader of his business unit and asked him about going directly to the executive vice president of human resources. His leader suggested a different approach. This began a series of escalations to other departments. With each conversation, Josh felt that people were giving him the runaround, but he did not give up. He began going above the heads of anyone who wasn't listening or being helpful. He finally spoke to someone in HR who could help. She explained that the health plan at the company was created by a benefits design team. When Josh asked to speak to the team, she told him that the team didn't talk to employees.

But by this time "no" wasn't registering with Josh. He insisted on a meeting and let the HR employee know he would continue up the chain of command until he got one. He reminded her of two important tenets of their company: always do the right thing, and embrace innovation. He pleaded, "My wife is dying. We have three young children to raise, and she's slipping away day by day. The *right thing* to do is to help our family. Yes, this HSCT treatment is radical; that's why the insurance doesn't want to cover it. But it is also successful, so granting coverage would be *embracing innovation*. That is what we do here."

His plea must have worked, because a few days later Josh got a call. The director of the benefits design team had agreed to meet with him. He had a week to prepare. Josh being Josh, he went online and looked at all the available plans our insurance company offered in the individual market to see if any of them covered HSCT. He did this because he simply did not believe that they had never in their history covered HSCT for autoimmune diseases like multiple sclerosis.

Pretty quickly, Josh discovered that there *were* plans that covered HSCT, so he began looking for examples of plans that covered it for autoimmune diseases. Then he hit the jackpot: examples of multiple plans that had wording supportive of coverage of HSCT for autoimmune diseases. After verifying what he had found with a few other sources, Josh began to look for evidence that the insurance company had covered the procedure in multiple regions of the United States. He found individual plans available in the four regions of the United States covering the treatment.

Josh kept this research quiet. He didn't want to raise false hopes in any of us, so he just printed out the example plans he had found and brought them to his meeting with the benefits design director.

In the meantime, my parents and I were getting serious about preparing to go to Italy. The scariest part for me was the prospect of not being able to communicate with the hospital staff. Dr. Saccardi spoke English, but how was I going to tell the nurses when I was in pain? How would I describe symptoms to them? We started desperately trying to learn Italian. My mom had a friend who had lived in Italy for a few years, and she came to their house weekly to practice with them. Josh's cousin who had lived in Italy gifted me the Pimsleur Italian language CDs to help me pick up anything I could. We were all in an Italian crash course.

My parents also put together a care schedule to make sure someone was with me at all times. We mapped out when my mom, dad, and Josh would fly to Italy, and my mother even purchased her tickets. She would be the one to travel to Florence with me.

While we were studying Italian and making our schedule, Josh was doing his own preparations for his meeting with the benefits design director. The day finally arrived, and they met for about an hour. Josh explained the situation in detail and reviewed the various denials we had received from the insurance company. He explained that the swiftness with which the denials had come led him to believe that they were predetermined. He explained how my doctor in Seattle had spent weeks painstakingly crafting a fifty-plus-page appeal, only to have it rejected within an hour of being submitted. He told the director about hiring an attorney to help us with the appeals process, and about exhausting all of our appeals and considering litigation, even though the chances of winning in court were slim. He then showed her the insurance plans he had found that covered HSCT for autoimmune diseases, evidence that the insurance company's claims that insurance companies had never covered the procedure for my condition were false. In fact, the insurance plans that Josh produced showing coverage of HSCT were being sold by the insurance company that administered the employer plan at Josh's company.

Josh left the meeting unsure of the outcome, but he knew he had presented a solid case. Whatever happened next, at least he had tried everything he possibly could.

Shortly before I was scheduled to fly to Italy, Josh called me at my parents' house.

"Are you sitting down?" he asked.

"Yes, why?" I replied.

"The insurance company wants to cover your treatment, and they want you to get it done in Seattle."

I could not believe my ears. I thought he was making it up. But I realized that not even Josh, with his twisted sense of humor, would joke about something this important. This was the miracle we had been praying for. What made it even more miraculous was that I had had no idea Josh had been working so hard to fight for my case. I was in shock. I rushed down the hall to tell my parents the news. They were dumbfounded. We just sat there staring at each other in disbelief. A few words were stammered, then almost in unison, we breathed a huge sigh of relief. I would get my treatment in Seattle.

ᘓ · ᘓ · ᘓ

Like all married couples, Josh and I don't always see eye-to-eye on everything. Multiple sclerosis has tested our marriage many times, and in the weeks and months to come we would encounter a whole new universe of challenges to our relationship. But the perseverance he showed in advocating for me even in the face of countless closed doors tells you everything you need to know about Josh and how he feels about me and how he approaches life. After so many crushing disappointments, he fought the fight we *had* to win to even have a chance at the real fight. What he did was nothing short of a miracle. I love him for many reasons, but I would never forget this one, even when his behavior didn't make sense to me—which it soon wouldn't.

8

THE SIGN

As impractical as it sounds, we went on a family vacation right before my treatment began. We had long ago scheduled a trip to Hawaii with Josh's sister and brother, their partners, and their kids—a total of fourteen people. Now that I had such limited time before temporarily moving to Seattle, I wanted to cancel the trip. This was the last week we would have our nuclear family together before my treatment split us up to go in four different directions. I wasn't sure I wanted to share that precious time with extended family.

But Josh wouldn't hear of cancelling the vacation. In retrospect, his insistence makes some sense. I later learned there had been three concerns driving his decision, concerns he couldn't share with me at the time. His heaviest concern was that I might die during the transplant. If we took this trip, he reasoned, the kids would have one last good memory with me that he hoped could counterbalance their hellish memories of the year we'd just been through. He wanted them to think of their mom lounging by a pool instead of crying in bed.

His second concern was that, if the transplant didn't work, my current condition would be our new normal, and he didn't want my disability to define our family. It was still important for the kids to travel and have fun. It was not that he didn't understand my desire to stay home when I felt like crap. He knew I found it humiliating going through the airport in a wheelchair. But at this point, if I never did things that were difficult for me, what kind of life would that be for our family?

There was a third concern that I know was going through his stubborn mind, because Josh and I are very similar in this way. He thought that if we just acted as if everything were normal and we kept moving forward, everything would somehow be okay. It was the same reason that had kept me at my job for so long. We didn't give up on something just because it was hard. That is not how we ever operated. When you give up, it's all over. At that point, Josh was still going forward with this mindset, while I had slipped into "just stay alive" mode.

The trip to Hawaii solidified in my mind what I had heard from experts all along: MS is a family disease. It was affecting my family almost as much as it affected me. I was disabled, Josh had to do the work of two parents, and my kids were desperate to help in any small way they could. Instead of being excited about a trip like children in a normal family would be, they were concerned about their mom.

Although my children were becoming strong, competent, empathetic people, it was not fair that they had continuous worries about their mother.

Josh did amazing work to ensure the trip was as easy and comfortable for me as possible. I greatly appreciated it, but there were times when the humiliation of the situation was unavoidable. I had a wheelchair, which made a great difference because I so easily became tired walking. But it was hard to remember that the chair always needed someone to push it, and occasionally I ended up having to move it myself, leaving me discouraged and even more exhausted.

Even with me struggling along beside them, my family had a great time. One of the days I even made it out to the ocean with them. For that afternoon, my pain was diminished and we had fun riding the waves. I wish the whole trip had been that way and that I could tell you wonderful stories about it, but the reality was that that day was only time I felt able to join any of the group activities. The experience of the trip made it painfully obvious that even the people around me day in and day out could not truly understand my situation. They could not be with me in that space, and I never wanted them to.

☉·☉·☉

On the flight home from Hawaii, nine-year-old Marin and I held hands the entire time. When we got off the plane, she would go home with her aunt. It turned out that the physical pain I had been experiencing was nothing compared to what happened to my heart at that moment. My children are a part of me; they were my reason to stay alive through this torture. Watching Marin walk away from us at the airport brought me to my knees as I sobbed.

When I finally pulled myself together, I had to say goodbye to Josh. We had decided it would be easiest for the two young ones if I stayed with them at my parents' house, their new home, for the few days I had before my departure to Seattle. I was going home with my parents, and Josh was going alone to our family home.

I spent my last three days with Noah and Hannah (ages six and three), reassuring them that this would not be forever. The time I was gone would fly by and they would have a wonderful time running around on the farm with their grandparents. We snuggled a lot. On my last night there, I kissed them goodnight for the last time and cried myself to sleep with them in my arms.

The next morning, when my dad and I were due to leave for Seattle, I woke up vomiting. I panicked. Would this mean my treatment would be postponed? We had invested so much time and effort to get to this moment. I was not sure I could take another disappointment. After a brief discussion we packed up to go anyway. "If you don't ask, the answer is always no. Let's drive up and hope that they start your treatment," my dad said. My endlessly thoughtful mother turned the front seat of the car into a bed complete with pillow and blanket, and I slept on the six-hour drive.

My dad woke me up as we pulled into the hotel parking lot. Again we stayed at the hotel a few short blocks from the clinic. We checked in and my father grabbed a luggage cart to get my many bags to the room. I was going to be there for a long time, through two seasons. I had packed enough clothes to keep me comfortable through whatever was ahead—weather-wise and health-wise.

Before we unpacked, we looked the room over carefully. During my time here, my immune system would be completely destroyed. We could not risk the possibility of an infection, so Josh had specifically requested a sterile room when he made the reservation.

"Do you smell that?" my father asked. There was a distinct smell of mildew. He picked up the phone and asked for a change of rooms.

The new room was better in every way. It smelled clean and was much larger. The best part came when we stepped out onto the balcony, which the previous room hadn't had. As we stood there, we could see a large red glowing sign: Seattle Cancer Care Alliance. It was a literal sign of hope.

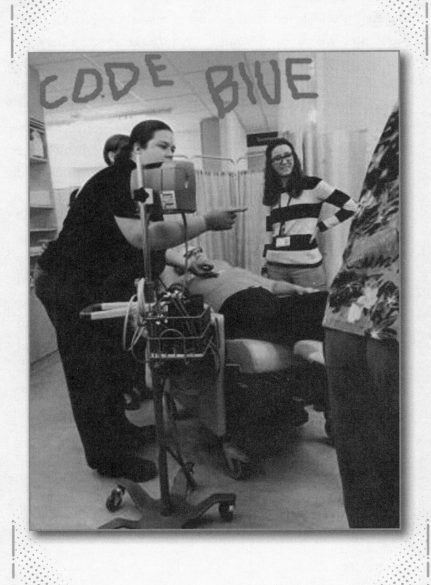

9

A COLONY OF ANTS

When I woke up the next morning, I had to peer out the window to see if my "sign of hope" was still there. I felt so positive about finally being here: next door to SCCA, an accepted patient, and facing my first day of HSCT. Whatever had caused my vomiting the day before had run its course. I felt much better, and I knew I was where I needed to be and ready for whatever came next.

On that crisp February morning my father and I had breakfast and chatted a little about what we expected out of the first day. We stepped out of the hotel and looked up at the clinic. The distance was short, but the grade was steep. "Are you sure you don't want me to get the car?" my father asked. I thought about it for a minute, but decided I wasn't ready to rely on the car just yet. I knew that would be in my future, but I wanted to walk as long as I possibly could. This turned out to be a decision I would grapple with every day, as that hill literally stood between me and the treatment we had fought so long to get. I linked my arm through my dad's to keep me straight and balanced and began walking. Halfway up there was a lamp post that would become my common resting spot.

When we got to the clinic, we were directed to registration. Here I signed a consent form, got my schedule, and found out I was still on the Gold Team. Being on the Gold Team made me happy. I had done what they suggested at my first visit and blinged out my folder with the help of my kids. The schedule for the week, however, did not make me happy. All I would be doing was meetings, blood work, and more testing. Knowing the first step in HSCT was to make my body produce stem cells, I was hoping that *something* would start in the first week. But no—just more tests.

After my Day 1 appointments, I was surprised to find I still had some energy. My dad and I decided to visit a Goodwill store three blocks from the hotel. Our hotel cupboard was missing two must-have items: a Scotch glass for him and a wine glass for me. I found the perfect specimen: a glass emblazoned with the word *Princess* and covered with crown-shaped rhinestones. I was so tickled with it I posted a picture on Facebook to let my friends and family know I still had a sense of humor.

Energy. How quickly it can disappear. On the walk back from the store, I saw the cutest black Labrador puppy. She was irresistible. I bent down to pet and play with her for just a minute . . . and when I stood back up, I was drained. I stumbled to a nearby bench to rest.

I had hit "the wall." It was the same wall I had become familiar with while running marathons. I would run to the point where I felt I could not keep going. This wall, however, was not one I could push through mentally with my "one more step" mantra. This one was much stronger, and I had to succumb. Once again, I was reminded I was disabled.

Eventually I regained some strength, and we returned to our hotel room. I was definitely done for the day. As my father and I put our new glasses to use, Marin called me. When I answered, she could barely talk through her tears. She was missing me terribly. I tried to make her feel better by telling her it is always tough adjusting to a new situation. I told her that her aunt loved her and would snuggle her tonight. By the end of our conversation she had stopped crying. The separation was clearly going to be hard on the whole family. I hoped tomorrow would end better for both of us.

The second day at the clinic I was scheduled to have an EKG first, then see the oncologist who would go over all the gory details and risks of HSCT again, then finish the day with a chest X-ray in the afternoon. Although there were only three appointments planned, there were hours of waiting in between.

Because of some scheduling changes, I had my X-ray before meeting with the oncologist. The technician was surprised to hear I was in the HSCT program as an MS patient. As one might expect, most of the patients at SCCA were there for cancer treatments. As we chatted more, he told me there was research being done to consider HSCT as a possible treatment for HIV and AIDS, which I had not been not aware of. Again, I was amazed that this treatment was in use for many autoimmune diseases, yet so few people were aware of it.

As I finished up the conversation with the tech, he wished me good luck. "Good luck" is an odd thing to say to a person embarking on a life-threatening journey, I thought to myself. It was not as if I were about to take a math test. And what exactly would *bad* luck be? I knew he had good intentions, however, so I simply replied, "Thank you."

Next came the last and most important appointment of the day, the meeting with the oncologist. I had expected Dr. Georges, but was told he was seeing patients at a different hospital. The doctor on rotation was much rougher around the edges. He treated the conversation like a business interaction. He laid out the procedures and the risks bluntly. I wasn't prepared for his impersonal and matter-of-fact approach. I became extremely emotional—crying and shaking. The conversation brought on a panic attack, and a bad one at that. The doctor quietly told my father we could use the room as long as we needed to before he exited. We stayed there for half an hour while I recovered.

It wasn't hearing about the risks that put me over the edge that day. I already knew all the information the doctor had given me about the procedure. I had heard it all and I was ready for it. I had been ready for it for a year now!

The fact that I had to go over all the unpleasant details and consent to it all *again* was insulting. I had left my family behind and moved to Seattle for this. *Of course I fucking consented! Just get started already!*

Day 2 turned out to be more exhausting than Day 1. By the time we returned to the hotel, I was a wreck. I called my friend Erica, someone I often turned to for support. She had a calming effect. As always, talking to her helped me gather my thoughts. I came to two realizations during that conversation. First, I had come to Seattle feeling like a warrior and ready to start treatment right away. Even though I knew that wasn't realistic, I was not dealing well with the days of more waiting, more tests, and more forms. Being patient had never been one of my strong suits.

Secondly, Erica pointed out, I was acting as if I were on a vacation. Planning activities and trying to take advantage of being in a new city was inappropriate for this trip. What I needed to do was fully acknowledge that I was sick and allow myself to act like a sick person—rest, let people help me, and stop worrying that I wasn't taking advantage of my time here. It was typical of me to have unrealistic expectations of what I could accomplish. And that attitude was not doing me any favors right now.

Identifying these two issues helped me relax. I was able to sleep that night. I was lucky to have Erica in my life, and I made her an honorary Gold Team member.

I woke up the next day feeling rested, and all I had on my schedule was a full MRI that would yield an image of my brain and spine. This image would establish a baseline before the transplant, meaning my future MRIs would all be compared to this one. The hope was to see zero progression of the disease in subsequent MRIs. I had read that some people even improved after HSCT. Lesions have been reported to shrink over time. I crossed my fingers that maybe that would happen for me.

Walking through the glass doors of SCCA, I felt hopeful that I might finally have an easy day. Over the past fourteen years, I had had many MRIs and had rarely had any issues. This was going to be a piece of cake.

My dad and I made our way to the imaging room on the second floor. Once there, I was handed the usual clipboard of paperwork to fill out confirming I could not be pregnant and had no metal implants in my body. Then I was shown to a locker room where I changed into hospital scrubs and put on the non-slip socks. The last thing I put in the locker was my jewelry. The earrings were not a problem, but the cross I wore around my neck was. My fingers would not cooperate with the clasp, so I found the lab technician for help. I was ready.

I got the usual instructions from the technician as I got myself onto the table that slid into the giant tube: "It is important not to move," he said, and "It will be loud." He also asked me if I had a playlist on my phone. This was something new to me. For my past MRIs technicians had either played a radio station over the headphones or simply handed me earplugs. This hospital had the latest and greatest innovations!

As soon as the table began sliding into the tube, however, my old friends the irritants suddenly appeared. I felt as if a colony of ants were crawling under the skin on my legs. I fought the incredible urge to kick. It was almost impossible to hold still. Then an itching spread to my head and face. This was not the irritants however; it was simply the knowledge that I couldn't touch my face that brought on the itching.

Obviously, I did not want to ruin the test. I *had* to figure out a way to calm myself. Over thirty years of dealing with migraine headaches and MS pain, I had learned many tricks to alleviate pain and anxiety. I prayed. I chanted. I tried visualization. I imagined seeing the discomfort I was feeling blow away as smoke through my exhalations. Next I tried to picture myself on a beach, watching the waves roll in, then discovering a mossy path behind me leading to a pool of turquoise blue water, which I dove into. This was one of my more clearly defined visions and usually worked well. But all of these techniques were ineffective; I could not get my mind off the complete and overwhelming irritation.

As much as I didn't want to, I was forced to squeeze the alert ball the technician had put in my hand as I entered the machine. The ball was to be used only if you had a problem during the testing, and this definitely qualified as a problem.

As soon as I squeezed the ball, the table I was lying on slid out of the imaging tube. I thought if I could shake out my limbs and refocus maybe I could make this work. I asked the technician to start over. A few minutes into the second attempt, I was squeezing the damn ball again. The technician refused to try a third time, in spite of my begging. "Rachel, I'm not in the business of torture," he said, his voice kind but weary. "We'll try again tomorrow."

The disappointment of the failed MRI brought on another anxiety attack. The technician was concerned and insisted I check in with the Gold Team before I left. He walked me out to my father in the waiting room and told him to take me to the fifth floor. The nurses there put me in the triage room and gave me Ativan to ease my anxiety. Thankfully, it worked quickly. They also gave me a prescription and advised me to take another dose before my next MRI.

Josh arrived that evening to spend the weekend with us. It was a relief to see him. I was able to fall asleep easily that night, exhausted yet again by the emotional challenges of the day.

The next day I finally had that elusive "easy" day. After getting a good night's sleep and taking Ativan, I was able to complete the MRI with no problems.

The first week was over. Josh and I had a free weekend to explore Seattle. I had researched activities online and wanted to go to a nearby arboretum. After a week of being in one small exam room after another, I needed to be outside. I wanted fresh air. When we got to the arboretum I immediately felt calmer. Out of nowhere I found the energy to run. I ran over a mile, and it felt awesome. I hadn't run in so, so long.

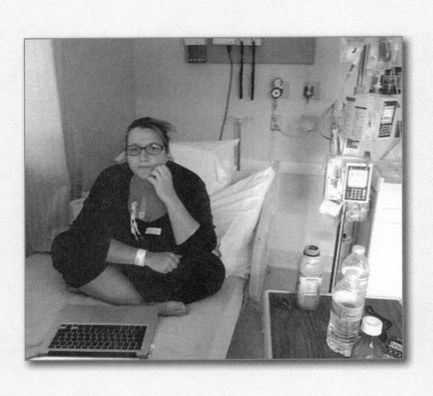

10

ONE DAY AT A TIME

*M*y *treatment wasn't just my treatment. It affected every member of my family. My parents, my children, and Josh were intermittently present with me as I went through it. This chapter is taken from the online message board we used to keep everyone informed of my progress. It includes some of my family's voices and perspectives. Note that Mike is my father and Margaret is my mother.*

Let's Get This Started!
Journal entry by Rachel — 3/4/2014

Today started early. We had back-to-back meetings all day. The staff drew blood and I peed in a cup for what felt like the millionth time; everything appeared normal.

At 9:15 we met with a nurse for baseline testing. This would establish my physical and cognitive state prior to HSCT. I could only hope for improvement after treatment. The nurse told me the results of my latest MRI: three new lesions on my brain, two of which were enhancing. I was in the middle of an exacerbation—no wonder I'd been feeling so crappy!

This news put Dad and me on edge. The nurse told us she didn't know how the exacerbation would affect the course of my treatment. She said it could be delayed, or they could start me on a new medication and wait for the exacerbation to calm down before we started. "I'm sorry," she said. "I really just don't know."

I wanted to press her for answers, to look her in the eye and say, "Do you have any idea how long I've been waiting?!" But I knew it was pointless, so I just sat silently while she left the room.

My appointment with the neurologist, Dr. Bowen, wasn't until 1:00, so I had over three hours to wait until I found out if and how this setback might affect my treatment plan. When I finally saw him, he said, "By Monday they should be harvesting some stem cells." I could have kissed him when he assured us there was no reason to change the schedule. The relief swept over me like a drug.

That relief lasted until the end of the day, when we met with the entire medical team. They informed us they had a new plan: start me on a form of chemotherapy called Cytoxan, then collect stem cells in about two weeks instead of in four days as the previous protocol had called for. They recommended this change because of my active lesions and because Dr. Georges had recently attended a conference and learned about the use of this drug to encourage the production of stem cells. Nothing like being on the cutting edge!

I was assured that this method would be less stressful for my body and more likely to yield all the stem cells needed on the first try, but . . . the process would be two weeks longer.

Before we were done with this long day of meetings, I met with a social worker. She offered to stop in to talk with me from time to time. Obviously, I like this idea. I'll be able to share things with her that I won't want to scare my parents or Josh with.

A Route Has Been Opened to Rachel's Heart!
Journal entry by Mike — 3/5/2014

The big activity Tuesday was getting a Hickman catheter. This is a semi-permanent tube that goes into the main vein right above the heart. The purpose is to allow various fluids to be administered into a large blood flow so they are well diluted. We spent most of the morning and part of the afternoon at the UW Health Center, three miles from the hotel. Rach was put almost under during the procedure. They call the form of anesthesia they used "twilight." She wasn't completely unconscious, but heavily sedated. The most important part is that she was unable to form new memories during twilight. It worked. She has no idea what happened, but she woke up with a tube sticking out of her chest.

Most of our time was spent waiting for her to wake up enough to be discharged. Now we are ready for Thursday, when she will get her first round of chemo.

Thursday, March 6 . . . Chemo
Journal entry by Mike — 3/6/2014

Today has been a hell of a day. We started at 1:30 this morning, when Rach woke me up because her dressing on the Hickman was becoming very painful. After fussing, fretting, and making phone calls, we ended up driving to the UW hospital to have the dressing changed. That was an adventure in itself. Back to the hotel room by 3:30, then up the hill to SCCA at 7:00 to get blood draws and begin the chemo infusion. The infusion turned out to be much longer than we had anticipated. The process started at 8:30 a.m., and we got back to the room at 9:30 p.m.

Josh got here this afternoon and is going to be the caregiver this weekend. I am going home to start care of the two little kids, and Margaret is going to fly up to start a two-week period here in Seattle.

Now that Rachel is actually started on the treatment, we have a pretty good idea of the timeline. If there are no unexpected diversions, such as infection, her treatment calendar is

3/6, started chemo (Cytoxan) and mobilization drugs (Neupogen).

3/7–3/15, getting sicker.

3/16– 4/6, recovering from chemo. This would be a good time to visit if you want to.

3/17–3/20, collect stem cells.

4/7–4/12, possibly start second round of chemo, called BEAM + ATG, which completely gets rid of old immune system.

4/14, transplant back her frozen stem cells.

4/24, engraftment, at which point the stem cells have entered the bone marrow and are producing a new immune system.

5/12–5/25, come home.

3/6/2015, get childhood inoculation, to educate the new immune system about some of the bad germs around.

This is just an educated guess at a schedule. Something is bound to knock it off a week or two.

Top Ten Chemo Symptoms, Day 1
Journal entry by Rachel — 3/7/2014

1. Nausea
2. Weakness
3. Difficulty walking
4. Extreme fatigue
5. Stars in my vision
6. Bloated and hard stomach (similar to pregnancy)

7. Burps, burps, and more burps
8. Feeling really crappy
9. Strong desire to back out of the whole thing
10. Remembering my worst cocktail hangovers
    ever

Do People Who Have Chemo Just Lie Around?
Journal entry by Josh — 3/8/2014

The last couple of days have been a challenge for Rachel due to the aftereffects of the surgery to install her Hickman line and the effects of the Cytoxan chemotherapy. She has managed to eat a little every day. We have also managed to keep on the 30+ pills a day she's required to take. In typical Rachel fashion, she continues to be a trouper.

It's hard to see her feeling bad about not getting up and accomplishing anything except daily trips up the hill to the hospital. She wondered out loud about other people who experience the "gift" of chemo. "Do people who have chemo just lie around?" she asked me many times today.

At this point, Rachel's daily hospital trips are primarily for blood draws to monitor her electrolyte levels and white blood cell (WBC) and red blood cell (RBC) counts; she'll also be getting Neupogen shots. Neupogen is a medication that will force her bone marrow to grow and release millions of stem cells from the marrow into her bloodstream quickly.

Today we were told that Rachel's WBC skyrocketed from 4,100 per microliter to over 21,000 per microliter. This indicates that the Neupogen is working as intended. In the next couple of days, they expect Rachel's WBC to start to decline to very low levels due to the chemotherapy. In about ten days, when her WBC is pretty much at its lowest, the bone marrow should start releasing the new stem cells. At that point they will collect and separate out the stem cells using a process called apheresis. They will hook the apheresis machine directly into her Hickman line and pull out her blood. This machine will spin the blood so fast the WBCs, plasma, and platelets will be sorted into different levels. The machine will then put the stem cells into a bag for storage and return the rest of the blood to her body.

There is so much to learn and remember.

Wheelchair Day
Journal entry by Josh — 3/9/2014

Just a quick update. This morning has been extremely rough for Rachel. She is very, very weak, and we are using a wheelchair today to get her around. We spent most of the morning at the hospital getting blood draws and Neupogen shots. Rachel's white cell and neutrophil count has started to drop from yesterday, which is what is expected. My MIL, Margaret, just arrived, and will be taking over as caregiver.

My Turn as Caregiver Begins
Journal entry by Margaret — 3/9/2014

I arrived around noon today. Josh and I had a brief time to exchange information before he had to get to the airport to fly home.

Rachel was so uncomfortable with constipation and gas that we called the triage nurse, who directed us to come into the hospital. Rach and I had a long wait at the hospital until she got an injection of something to get her guts moving, and even *more* pills. It was not an immediate fix; she was still in quite a bit of discomfort as we headed back to the hotel. We did find a few things to laugh and cry about. I am relieved that our Rachel's spirit is still here.

Several hours later, I am still looking at my bags to unpack, but Rachel and I ate and spent time together before she thought she might go to sleep. I'll have to wake her in an hour to give her the last round of meds for the day. The number of pills and medications Rachel has to take is staggering. I hope I don't screw it up!

A Better Day
Journal entry by Margaret — 3/10/2014

Today was definitely an "up" from yesterday's down. Rachel slept through the night, woke up on her own, took a shower, and was ready to go to the hospital by 9:00.

Once at the hospital there was a blood draw and a check-in with "Rainbow Rick," a nurse with 30 years of experience in the transplant arena. His nickname refers to the fact that he works with all the different color teams.

Rick changed the dressing on Rachel's Hickman line, which was very painful and continues to bother her. Her blood counts were about normal but will go down from here. We'll have to start taking her temperature twice a day because infection is now such a danger.

After her appointments, we did laundry at the hotel and, amazingly, Rachel had the energy to walk to the corner drug store. I bought prune juice to help Rachel's digestion. Is prune juice really that awful? Rachel thinks so!

It was a pretty big day, but a good one. Given how many tough days there are ahead, we felt thankful.

White Cell Count Dropping
Journal entry by Margaret — 3/11/2014

Rachel's WBC count is dropping—and that's a good thing!

Although this puts Rach in more jeopardy of infection, it is necessary to produce new cells, which, theoretically, have no MS memory. We look forward to a harvest of cells at the end of this week or early next week.

In the meantime we take our daily trips to the hospital and evaluate Rachel's energy level afterward to see what else we might fit into the day. Today we walked over to a shopping area and had lunch. By the time we got back to our hotel, her energy was sapped.

A side note, and another ironically good sign, is that Rachel had severe bone pain this afternoon, caused by new stem cells being released through the bone into the bloodstream.

Rachel is in good spirits as the treatment follows what is expected and moves ever closer to the uphill climb.

White Cell Count Dropping
Journal entry by Rachel — 3/12/2014

Today I went to physical training for the first time. It's so funny to me to be basically starting over like a little kid—learning to sit down and stand up and lift my arms— especially after I've trained to run marathons. It makes sense, though. I can barely make it up a flight of stairs by myself.

After I got back to the hotel I thought I was feeling pretty good, but I was also very weak. I don't understand how it keeps surprising me that I end up so tired even though it happens every single day. I'm also about to become neutropenic, which means my WBC will be so low I can't risk going to confined places with strangers. Hopefully my WBC will be at the lowest tomorrow, and they can harvest this weekend.

I have mixed feelings about whether to be excited, scared, or panicked. Maybe all three are appropriate. It's just the way it's going to be for now.

This was the last journal entry I made. After this I simply got too sick to write.

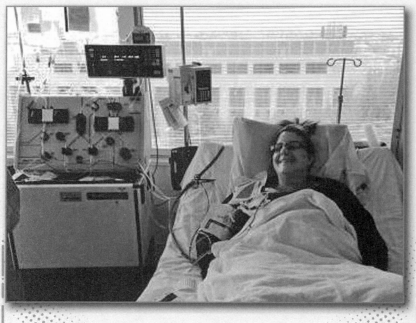

11

HARVEST, HAIR, AND HUNGER

The next three weeks were long and tedious as I waited for my body to produce enough stem cells to harvest. My schedule was pretty much the same every day. First we would walk or drive up the hill to SCCA for a blood draw and a dressing change for my Hickman line. Then I would take the elevator up to the sixth floor to meet with the Gold Team and have a shot to mobilize my stem cells. After that we would return to the hotel, where I would collapse. Regardless of which caregivers were with me or what visitors came and went, my life was ruled by this regimen.

I met with the same three members of the Gold Team daily. They were informative yet empathetic; under different circumstances, I would have chosen them as friends. They made me feel as if my treatment was the most important appointment of their day. While one of them took my vitals, another reminded me of the side effects of the chemotherapy: sores in my mouth, bone and joint pain (caused by bones releasing stem cells into the bloodstream), hair loss, and fatigue. Somehow they managed to make all of these miseries sound normal.

One morning when my appointments started later in the day than usual, I crawled into bed with my mother to enjoy coffee while watching one of our favorite shows on TV. As I took my first sip, I felt a stab of pain on the roof of my mouth. I ran my tongue over the painful spot and realized I had an open sore there. I knew the first sign of the chemo would be sores in the mouth. After waiting for what felt like months for signs of the effects of the treatment, I was giddy. Something was finally happening!

When my mom and I arrived at SCCA, I felt unusually weak and lightheaded. And I was nauseated on top of that. The blood draw that day showed that I was now neutropenic as well. (Another step toward the stem cell harvest!) A nurse explained that even though the chemo was technically out of my system, it was still killing off my cells. The combination of my cells dying and my being neutropenic was making me weaker than usual. This was all part of creating the conditions necessary to produce new cells that had no MS memory.

I also found out that the sores in my mouth likely continued all the way down my esophagus, explaining my nausea. My nasal passages were also feeling raw. All of my mucus membranes were dying. I had the feeling this was going to be just the tip of the iceberg.

But once again, this would not be the day they would start harvesting my stem cells.

It was always disappointing to return to the hotel still in waiting mode, but Mom made it better by making an extra soft chocolate chip cookie that melted in my mouth. Feeling taken care of can make any day a little better.

As predicted, next on the list of side effects were bone and joint pain. I was jolted awake at 3:00 a.m. by excruciating pain. When I tried to walk I felt as if my skeleton would not support me. The pain encompassed the entire area from my hips to my knees. As I tried to assess where the pain was generating from, I imagined my bones were burning red under my skin, irritated and inflamed. I knew there was no chance the pain would relent; I had taken six oxycodone, two more than the suggested limit. We called the SCCA triage nurse, who said there was nothing more to do except take two Tylenol. This seemed so ridiculous I wanted to laugh, but I was in too much pain.

I had encountered the sores in my mouth and the bone and joint pain. Now I waited for my hair to fall out and for more severe fatigue to complete the menu of expected side effects.

☙•☙•☙

It had to happen sooner or later: our first "Code Blue."

Josh was the one lucky enough to be with me at the time. He had arrived in Seattle the night before and had witnessed the misery of my bone and joint pain. When we got to the clinic for the morning blood draw, I was completely wiped out. As the phlebotomist prepared to take my blood, I told her I was lightheaded. Having just taken my blood pressure, she said that she was not surprised, since my blood pressure was very low. She calmly continued preparing for the draw. She didn't seem concerned, so I wasn't either. But as the blood flowed, I grabbed Josh's arm and whispered, "I don't feel right." I was dizzy, and everything was going dark. It wasn't long until I was no longer whispering. "I think I'm going to pass out!" I shrieked.

This crisis was attended by two doctors, a hospital administrator, two physician assistants, three nurses, a note-taker, and two social workers. They all seemed to appear out of nowhere. Someone rolled in a crash cart—a portable set of drawers with life-saving medicines and equipment. The room filled with an overwhelming energy that brought on an anxiety attack. Twenty-five minutes and a great deal of discussion later, I was moved to the triage room on the sixth floor, where I was hooked up to an IV for rehydration, more painkillers, and anxiety medication. Slowly my world changed from fear and chaos to something closer to normal. What the heck had happened? Josh and I had plenty of time to speculate about the effects of pain, drugs, emotions, fear, and anxiety on one human body. On that day, the combination added up to Code Blue.

By mid afternoon I was back in the hotel room, where I took a long nap. When I woke up, life was miraculously back to normal. A Seattle friend visited; my mom, Josh, and I ate a nice dinner; Josh walked to the drug store. Aside from a little Code Blue, it was just another day in Seattle.

But from now on it was never a question whether I would walk or drive up the hill; I was now capable only of being a passenger. After the Code Blue incident, I decided I didn't need to push myself to tears and exhaustion every day. I didn't need to walk places. I simply needed to make it to the harvest.

☺·☺·☺

Each day I hoped that my blood count would be high enough for harvesting stem cells, but I remained guarded so as not to be disappointed when the answer was no. The doctors wanted to get enough cells the first time rather than doing the harvesting over two days. The target number for the harvest was four million. Can you imagine the technology necessary to accurately count four million cells?

Eventually, much to my joy, my blood test results came back with flying colors! Finally, it was harvest day. I felt like Dorothy finally meeting the Wizard of Oz.

We didn't even have time to celebrate. By the time I got to the Gold Team after giving blood, they already had my results and ushered me straight to the room where the harvesting would take place. I sat in a large gray recliner next to a huge machine that looked as if it belonged in a sci-fi movie: the apheresis machine. It was strange to watch my blood flow out and back into my body; I felt nothing. The blood came out of the Hickman line in my chest and went into a centrifuge. This futuristic machine spun my blood fast enough to separate it into three layers: the red cells settled at the bottom, the plasma went to the top, and the stem cells stayed in a pocket in the middle. For four hours the machine whirled and swirled. At the end, the lab technician siphoned the stem cells off and collected them in bags. It all seemed so amazingly simple.

Even though I was looking forward to having my cells harvested, that evening was emotionally rough. I don't know if it was all the meds I was on, the stress, the MS, or all of the above, but I was anxious. Did they get enough stem cells? Would I have to go through the process again?

Luckily, the next morning I got the news that my stem cell harvest had exceeded expectations. They counted seven million stem cells—three million more than they needed! Josh, my mom, and I celebrated with a lunch out.

I allowed myself to revel in the joy of feeling halfway decent and happy that day. Those moments were few and far between, and I forgot how great it can be simply not to be in severe pain. The phantom burning was finally reduced to the point of being tolerable. The last few days had been full of good news, and I felt encouraged. On my next visit to SCCA, the team informed me that my platelets were looking so good I would not need a blood transfusion. My white blood cell counts were climbing, which meant I could be less cautious of germs. Even better, I no longer had daily appointments. From here on out I would be seen weekly until this round of chemotherapy was out of my system. These milestones felt huge.

To mark the progress, we had a beauty shop day. My mom picked up some pink fingernail polish and scissors to cut my long hair. I wanted a transitional look before my hair fell out. I even put on makeup, and we went to the Chihuly Garden and Glass exhibit near the Space Needle after the doctor appointments. It was a great day.

☺•☺•☺

After so much activity I was ready for a good night's sleep, but when I got into bed, I couldn't relax. I got up and ate a bowl of Greek yogurt with a packet of instant oatmeal. Then I ate a medicated brownie. This was after a filling dinner, two bowls of ice cream, and a bowl of pudding. I couldn't stop eating. I had been warned this was a side effect of the high doses of steroids I was taking, but I wasn't prepared for the ravenous compulsion I felt.

The next morning my first thought was of food. I went to the kitchen and made myself oatmeal. My mom saw what I was doing and reminded me that I was supposed to wait an hour after taking my morning pills before eating. I heard her, but when she handed me the pills I took them and immediately ate my oatmeal anyway. My mom asked me if I had not heard her or if I was just ignoring her, but I couldn't answer. I honestly didn't know. After getting dressed

I went to the hotel breakfast bar and proceeded to eat even more: two waffles topped with whipped cream, blueberries, walnuts, strawberries, and chocolate chips. Then I grabbed two muffins for the walk back to the room. I did not enjoy this drive to eat. I prayed that when I started to taper down the prednisone, I would get better at controlling this never-satisfied hunger.

After the never-ending breakfast, we went to an appointment at SCCA, during which my mom had her second supervised lesson in flushing my Hickman line. Now that I didn't have daily appointments, my caretaker would be responsible for that duty. Flushing the Hickman line, protecting me from germs, and administering an ungodly number of pills was a heavy burden on whoever was helping me. My mom was terrified she would kill me with one goof-up.

☙ • ☙ • ☙

At our last meeting with the Gold Team for a few days, the nurses commented that it looked like I would have to wait until my next round of chemo for my hair to fall out. Might there be one expected chemo side effect I would not have?

The steroids boosted my energy level, so I was able to take walks. My mom and I had walked past a great-looking Thai restaurant several times, and we decided to treat ourselves to lunch there. As we chatted about how to spend this break from daily hospital visits and how much I missed my kids, I started messing around with the back of my hair. Then I noticed my mom was staring at the white plate in front of me. I looked down to see ten or so hairs on the plate. Then I realized I was holding a handful of hair.

No matter how long you've expected it or how mentally prepared you think you are, having your hair fall out is a monumental event for a woman. It is impossible to imagine how it will feel to have your physical being change in such a drastic way. I had a minor freak-out, but calmed myself by remembering that this was part of this process.

Long ago I had decided to get my head shaved when my hair started falling out. I did not want to be obsessively pulling at my hair or finding it on my pillow every morning. One thing we discovered, in this area with so many chemotherapy patients, was that the gift shops and hair salons catered to the needs of bald women. The salons offered free shaves and henna tattoos. The gift shops had beautiful hats and scarves to offer alternatives to a cold, bald head. I would go back and forth on the question of being brave enough to just go around bald. I had already started a cap and scarf collection to make sure I had something to match any outfit.

Our Thai lunch conversation quickly shifted to getting to a hair salon. There happened to be one across the street from our hotel that offered free shaves. After finishing lunch, we made our way there. The hairdresser had done this many times and had a developed a sensitivity regarding women losing their hair. To lighten the mood, she started by giving me a Mohawk. My mom took multiple pictures of me in crazy poses before the final shave took place. Within twenty minutes I had gone from a full head of hair to a rocker Mohawk to a totally bald head.

Prior to this, all the symptoms of my illness had been invisible. Now there was a clear, physical sign that I was sick. I thought I was prepared, but it was still quite a shock. My mom and I crossed the street to the hotel arm in arm, went up the elevator to our room, and plopped down on the couch where we proceeded to watch movies and cry.

I had always been proud of my thick, silky hair, and the emotional impact of losing it exhausted me; I slept soundly that night. My mother finally woke me at 11:00 the next morning. She didn't want me to start out too far behind on my pain medications. It was never a good day when my pain was not under control from the beginning.

After I got up and took my meds, I looked in the mirror. Instead of the warrior I was hoping to see, I saw a bald, pale, puffy-cheeked, middle-aged, sick woman carrying forty extra pounds. I decided the first thing I needed to do, after getting some coffee, was to make this alien face look more like me. I put on makeup, got dressed, and picked out a cute cap to wear. Plenty of eye makeup and lipstick later, I was really starting to like this look. Plus, I realized how much time I would save each morning not having to style my hair. Despite all these attempts to stay positive, I felt sad every time I saw my reflected self without a head covering.

When my head was exposed I felt the chill of the air on my scalp. It was unfamiliar and uncomfortable. But if I wore a hat my head got too hot. I needed to rotate through three or four hat thicknesses throughout the day. At least it was an excuse to shop!

The next step toward normalizing my new look was to show my kids. When I called them that morning I used FaceTime so they could see me. To ease them in, I started with a scarf on. How would they react to their mother being bald? I was relieved that they were genuinely curious and wanted to see under the scarf right away. As I unwrapped my head, I felt a horrible panic coming on. How could I make this seem fun, interesting, and special? To me, it just felt wrong. But I shouldn't have underestimated my children's ability to see beyond the baldness and just see me. They asked how it felt and if they could touch my head when they came to Seattle. They confirmed for me that, bald or not, I was still Mommy.

☙·☙·☙

The next step of my treatment was a long hospital stay, when I would have more chemotherapy prior to receiving my disease-free stem cells. But before that I had a brief window of time during which my immune system was recovering from the first round of chemo but still strong enough for me to go out and be active. It felt like the perfect time to have all three kids come up for a visit.

I hadn't seen Marin, Noah, and Hannah for three weeks, and I was giddy with anticipation for their arrival. I picked out my best head scarf, a bright red one with sequins. Figuring I was about to experience a dog pile of little bodies on top of me for most of the day, I opted for a tank top to help offset the heat. One thing that made me nervous was the need to protect the Hickman line coming out of my chest. How could I prevent all three children from lunging at me in unison? But the worry was for nothing. The hugs and smooches created no problems, and their affection was the best thing I'd felt in a long time. We had a lovely reunion playing at the park across the street and later snuggling in the hotel room.

We had decided that the kids should experience the world-famous aquarium during their visit to Seattle. Luckily, I had enough energy to go. Josh called ahead and had a wheelchair waiting for me when we arrived. It was still embarrassing for me to be in a wheelchair in public, but it was better than missing out on that precious time with my children.

After exploring the aquarium, I was able to walk to lunch and then back to the car. Hannah, my youngest, was holding my hand and fiddling with my wedding ring as we crossed the street. Suddenly, she started crying and yelling at the same time. It took a moment to understand her. "Your ring! Your ring!" she cried. I looked down at my hand, panicked. Sure enough, my wedding ring was gone. "Where is it?" I asked Hannah, trying to keep my voice as steady as possible. I didn't want to scare her, but I could feel my throat closing up. She pointed down the street. "Back there!"

I immediately turned and started walking back down the street while Josh hustled the kids into the car. "Are you sure you have enough energy for this?" he asked as he strapped Hannah into her car seat. But at that point I had so much adrenaline pumping through my veins I could hardly hear him. I frantically retraced our path across the busy street, scouring the pavement with my eyes. I looked in every crack and cranny along the sidewalk, then returned to the car just as deliberately. After several passes, tears began streaming down my face. My ring was really gone. I wanted to look one more time, but Josh stopped me. He reasoned with me that it was a very busy street and he doubted it would ever be found. Later that evening I talked my mom into walking that block one last time, but we both knew it was mission impossible.

Why was losing my ring so hard for me to accept? In the scheme of everything I was going through it seems trivial. But to me it felt like yet another loss added to a list that was getting so long I couldn't bear it. I had lost my life as I once knew it. I had lost months with my kids. I had recently lost my immune system and my hair, and now I had lost my wedding ring. I would face the rest of my treatment without this symbol of some of my most important identities—those of wife and mother. I could grow back the stem cells and the hair, but I could never replace the ring my husband had given me on the day he promised to love me forever and never leave me.

You would think we had experienced enough excitement for one day, but later that evening, as my mom was showing Josh how to flush out my Hickman line, an attachment came unscrewed. We had a moment of panic as we called the triage nurse. She urged us to get to the hospital immediately. Josh grabbed the car key and we scrambled to put on our coats.

The detail of this story I remember most vividly is the huge bowl of rice pudding I was eating while all this was happening. I was still on my steroid-induced eating marathon at this point, and I refused to leave the pudding behind even as my heart was exposed to the world and potentially being contaminated. My mom did her best to reason with me, but I was like a woman possessed. So as Josh drove me to the hospital I was still shoveling pudding into my mouth.

The Hickman line episode was quickly resolved, but I'll never stop laughing—and cringing—at that memory.

�♡ • ♡ • ♡

Since Josh and the children were staying in Seattle for a few days, my mom flew home to spend some time with my dad before he came back to take over as caregiver. The hotel suite turned into a high-energy place—quite a shift from the regimented life I had been living there. It was wonderful to have my kids with me, but it was also tough.

We scheduled a family meeting with a child psychologist during my weekly SCCA checkup. In this meeting the psychologist walked the kids through my entire procedure in language children could understand. Each child was able to flush a Hickman line on their own "patient," a new stuffed animal they chose from a large pile. As expected, Noah went straight for the turtle, his favorite animal. After that, the kids went to my regular appointments with me and got to meet the Gold Team.

At those visits, I learned that I was continuing to do well despite the many side effects of the numerous medications I was on. And I finally got an admission date to the University of Washington Medical Center (UW) to start the transplant! April 5, just a week away. At last we could start planning for the near future. On the admission day, I would start the BEAM chemotherapy. (BEAM is an acronym representing the four chemotherapy drugs used.) For three or four weeks, I would be an inpatient at UW. After being discharged, I would stay in Seattle for another two to three weeks to ensure the transplant was successful and that I was healthy enough to go home.

Oh, the best laid plans!

Two days later, my kids went home. My father returned as caregiver, and the hotel suite was quiet again. On one of the remaining days before my admission to UW, we decided to go shopping. Despite bringing what I thought was enough clothes with me, I found that I didn't really have the right clothes. For example, I wish someone had told me to pack V-neck shirts. I hadn't realized I would have a tube sticking out of my chest that medical staff would have to access daily. I also needed clothing I could layer to help me manage the hot flashes I was now having due to being on so many medications. While we were at Goodwill, I decided to look for a fake wedding ring. I felt naked without a ring on my finger. With the many difficulties I knew were ahead of us once I had the transplant, I didn't want anything else to feel uncomfortable. I found one with plenty of bling for only five dollars.

On one of our other days of free time, we went for a walk in the arboretum next to Lake Washington. UW rents canoes and rowboats, and we decided to take advantage of the beautiful day. We rowed around watching the bufflehead ducks nervously eyeing the bald eagles circling overhead. I felt almost normal.

Monday I had a couple of morning appointments to get me ready for my admission to the hospital. The plan was to begin the heavy BEAM chemo the day I was admitted. They would continue administering a series of the four drugs over the next six days, completely killing off my immune system. By April 11, I would be ready to get my new immune system "seeded" with the seven million frozen stem cells that had been collected. Those little buggers would migrate into my bone marrow and begin pumping out a brand-new set of healthy white blood cells.

After the Monday morning appointments, we had no reason to be in Seattle until Friday, so we took a road trip. This was my last opportunity to leave Seattle for weeks. I had grown weary of the hotel-SCCA routine, and I wanted to see my kids in their current homes. We zigzagged from Seattle to Vancouver to the Oregon coast to the Cascades. I was terrified I would catch germs from my kids, so there was lots of hand sanitizer and no kissing. Getting sick at this point could bring my treatment to a halt. Hell, with my diminished immune system, it could kill me. I had come way too far to let a cold germ do me in.

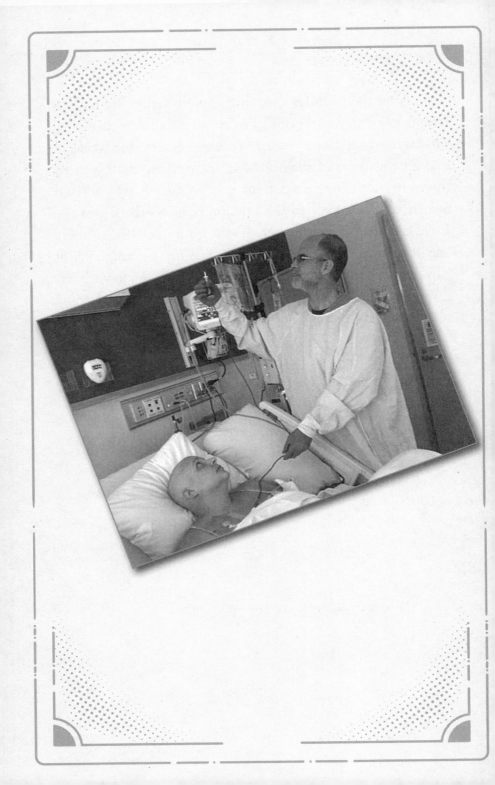

12

BIRTHDAY PARTY

Taking a road trip right before starting intensive chemotherapy probably wasn't the smartest plan, but I had to take the opportunity to see and touch my children. I was about to be sealed away in a hospital for at least three weeks, maybe more.

And that was the best-case scenario.

During the trip, the fact that I might die during HSCT—that this might be the last time I saw my family—was always at the back of my mind. After such emotional visits, the six-hour ride back to Seattle was grim, and not only because I was entirely depleted. I started throwing up again. This was exactly what I had feared, but there was nothing to do but keep moving forward, literally and figuratively.

Thankfully, my nausea was gone the next day. My father put the bag I had carefully packed in the car, and we drove to the UW hospital. During admission, I told the nurse about being sick the day before. She said my episode sounded like steroid withdrawal; I had been tapering off of them, but apparently not slowly enough. My treatment could go forward as planned.

With that potential setback behind me, I was ready to take on a week of chemotherapy. If all went according to plan, I would start off with BEAM, a high-dose chemotherapy regimen used to destroy the T-cells (my misguided white-cell soldiers). Then, to kill off any remaining T-cells, I would have anti-thymocyte globulin (ATG) administered. Years ago researchers had learned that they could grow ATG more quickly in rabbits than in larger animals, so that's what I was getting: "the rabbit treatment." After a week of these combined treatments, my immune system would be effectively dead and I would then be ready for my stem-cell infusion. The doctors referred to this as Day Zero. It was also referred to as a "birthday." I preferred to think of it as a celebration, so I decided to call it my birthday.

The hospital staff showed me to room 8210, where I took stock of my surroundings. It was a typical hospital room, although maybe a bit larger. It had a hospital bed in the center, a fake-wood free-standing closet, a small table, and a recliner that transformed into a bed. There was a television and even a window so I could look out and see the world. The bathroom was huge, with an open shower including a seat. The level floor meant I would not have to step in and out of a tub to bathe.

The first day of chemo was remarkably smooth, much to my surprise. I had been warned the side effects would be severe, but the nausea and fatigue I felt were nothing new.

For this brief period, I felt rather lucky. But over the next few days, things deteriorated. I was permanently hooked up to an IV that dripped fluids into my body, and the nurses swapped out the bags continuously. It was impossible to keep track of what was entering my bloodstream at any given moment. What I did know was that I was feeling increasingly anxious and emotional and that my bouts of nausea and vomiting were getting more difficult to control. Mornings started out relatively well, but as the day progressed things would go downhill. All of this was expected; the nurses told us every day that things would get worse before they got better. Yes, this was bad, but it was actually the calm before the storm.

Two days before my "birthday," I got the rabbit treatment. Despite the Disneyesque code words, it was really more like a Stephen King movie. Or, if you prefer the storm metaphor, we were about to experience a category five hurricane. ATG was the last drug that would enter my system before I received my new stem cells; its job was to finish destroying my immune system. We knew this agent was dangerous and harsh, but what happened was beyond what we could ever have imagined.

After it was over, Josh posted on CaringBridge, an online site where we were sharing my progress with family and friends. "I won't go into the details of the last 36 hours, but needless to say, I have witnessed the most difficult thing that anyone should ever have to go through." The hospital staff's description was "Reactions during rATG infusion: Severe acute diffuse pain and migraine. Fever during infusion. Rash." That's a clinical way of saying the treatment was excruciating. Josh was trying to protect me with the vagueness of his post, and the hospital staff wrote up what happened in the most clinical way possible for my file. I thought about writing something equally vague or medicalese here. But, knowing that some readers may be making decisions about this treatment, I want to be honest—and embarrassingly clear—about what happened during this time.

To start with, I didn't just have a rash; the pain I had almost blinded me. I was clearly allergic to something in the medicine.

As bad as that was, there was worse. When Josh called my mother to report the effects of the rabbit concoction on my body, he kept repeating the phrase "Rachel soiled herself" as my mother tried to get further details. What Josh was too embarrassed to put into words was that I was having diarrhea in my pants and in bed. I woke up in the night aware that I felt wet but was too exhausted and disoriented to understand what was happening. When the nurse came to check on me, I was filthy. As soon as she woke me up, I started vomiting. I was now losing it out of both ends. The pain, cramping, and nausea were compounded by the worst shame and humiliation I have ever experienced. I tried to get up and get to the toilet, but I couldn't stop anything from coming out. I literally made a trail on the floor behind me.

In the bathroom I tried to clean myself as best I could—which wasn't very well. My poor husband rushed to help. He was trying to clean up the trail I had left, but the nurse shouted, "Stop!"

"No, I can help!" Josh insisted.

"You are exposing yourself to the chemo. You need to stop right now," the nurse said sharply. "I'm prepared for this. You're not."

Josh reluctantly let her finish cleaning the mess. She was right. We were not prepared for this.

☺ · ☺ · ☺

With the hell of the rabbit treatment still in full swing, it was almost funny when the nurses handed Josh a brochure titled "Preparing for Your Cryopreserved Stem Cell Infusion" that outlined all the possible side effects of the next foreign agent being put into my bloodstream. For storage, the stem cells were combined with a preservative called dimethyl sulfoxide (DMSO). The DMSO could cause a number of unpleasant symptoms, most of which I had already experienced in the last week: nausea, stomach cramps, allergic reaction. The only one that was new was that the preservative might cause a funny taste in my mouth, so my mom loaded up on fruit candies and mints.

The night before my transplant, I actually slept. My rash was subsiding, and my nausea and diarrhea were finally under control. From the outside, I looked better. On the inside I still felt pretty terrible, but at least I wasn't shitting myself. Josh was sorry to miss out on the actual infusion of my new cells, but he had to leave early that morning. That left my mom and me alone for this monumental event.

The "birthday" was scheduled for 1:00 p.m. As the hour approached, our anticipation became almost overwhelming. Right on time, the transplant tech rolled in with the frozen packets of my precious harvested cells, a large sink for warming them to body temperature, and a supervisor to ensure the procedure was done correctly. I would be injected with two bags of stem cells; each bag would take ten to twenty minutes to administer. After the ATG episode, we all worried about another allergic reaction, but there was no turning back now. All we could do was stay the course and pray.

The drip began at 1:16 exactly. Everyone in the room was on full alert for any negative reactions or side effects. By 1:26 the first bag was empty of all the hopeful cells. At 1:29, after the second bag began to drip, I started to feel nauseated and my throat became unbearably hot. The nurse slowed down the infusion, and my symptoms subsided.

By 1:39, seven million of my preserved stem cells had reentered my body. The whole team clapped and yelled, "Happy birthday!" In that moment, it really did feel like a celebration. We had been waiting for this moment for almost two years.

I don't remember what happened next. Everything that follows was reported to me.

My mom was live-journaling the transfusion. She noticed a flushed area on either side of my face and, being the artist she is, even drew a small sketch of it in her journal. At about 1:50, I tried to tell her something, but she couldn't understand me. When she came closer and asked me to repeat myself, she realized that my speech was slurred and I wasn't making any sense.

The birthday party was over.

One in Two Thousand
Journal entry by Margaret — 4/11/2014

As the medical team and I whooped and clapped at the success of the infusion, I saw that Rachel's lips were moving. I leaned down to hear what she was saying and could make out only the word husband *intermingled with a lot of slurred sounds and then silence. This took place in what seemed like a nanosecond. I yelled for help. Room 8210 erupted into a flurry of phone calls and an army of staff crashing through the door.*

Quickly Rachel's bed was being wheeled out the door. I frantically chased the bed down the hall, trying to keep up. The bed was pushed into the elevator by the surrounding staff and I inched my way in around the unfolding drama as the doors closed. We emerged onto the imaging floor, where I heard "wait here" as the bed was pushed through two swinging doors.

Scared and alone, I sat in a small waiting area. I could think of nothing useful to do. Both Josh and Mike, the main support team, were in cars with kids, so calling them without any useful information would only lead to potential panic. As

I sat there, however, my cell phone received a series of calls from Josh, who surmised that the infusion was over by now. I didn't answer the calls. I realized this was not the time to talk to him.

I called my sister to unload and share my distress over this frightening turn of events. She listened, comforted, and assured me that all I could do was wait. Eventually a nurse came out the double doors and explained that the CT scan had ruled out a brain bleed and that that was very good news. She also informed me that Josh had called and talked to the staff and now knew that things had not gone well. I dreaded calling him back because Rachel was still unconscious, but I had to now. I tried to speak in a calm manner, assuring him that I would call him as soon as there was more to share.

It wasn't too long before the swinging doors opened, the bed was pushed back into the elevator, and we returned to the eighth floor. Rachel lay there still totally out of it, and there was, as yet, no explanation for what had just happened. Then another trip down to the imaging floor—this time for an MRI. I was asked questions: Had she had seizures in the past? Did she have a history of any event like this? No and no.

Rachel was put in the ICU, and I sat watching and waiting for some indication that she was coming back to us. At 4:15 p.m., almost three hours after her transplant, Rachel began to come to. This was a tremendous relief, not only to me but to the medical staff as well. By now the doctors were talking about a seizure in the brain as a reaction to the preservative (DSMO). A catastrophic event such as a stroke was eliminated as a possibility. Throughout the evening, Rachel regained her strength on her right side, which had been the most affected by this episode. Her speech remained slurred.

We had just experienced a horrific scare—the closest to seeing my child die as I ever care to witness. All the sayings such as "expect the unexpected" and "take it one day/one minute at a time" did not prepare me for this experience.

Ultimately the doctors reported that they didn't see anything alarming on the MRI; they still wanted to have it reviewed by an expert, but they were convinced my "spell" had been a reaction to the DMSO. Since I was likely never going to have another transplant, they felt confident that this was a one-time episode. Apparently this type of reaction happens to one in two thousand patients. Normally I would joke at this and say, "Lucky me!" But at that point I didn't have many jokes left.

They never did find out exactly what had happened to me while I was unconscious. The official hospital report states, "She developed an acute neurologic deficit 15 min after the infusion was done. She had slurred speech, right side weakness and left gaze. She was moved to ICU and had spontaneous recovery few hours later. The CTA and MRI ruled out stroke and MS flare, so we believe that the reason for her acute neurologic issue was seizures from DMSO."

When I pushed for answers at my one year follow-up, Bernie, the study coordinator, told me there were seven different opinions from seven different doctors.

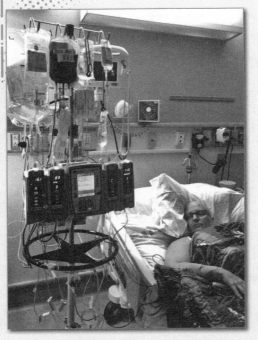

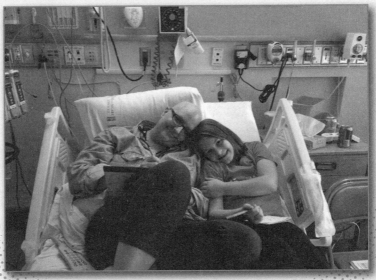

13

DOG DAYS

When we started on this journey, people had told us to "expect the unexpected" and "take it one minute at a time." I'd heard those expressions my whole life, but I never appreciated their full meaning until my time in room 8210.

An expression I had not heard before was "dog days," but that was how people described the days after a stem cell transplant. My dad wasn't familiar with the expression either, so, ever the researcher, he looked it up. The phrase originated in Greek and Roman times, in reference to the fact that Sirius, the Dog Star, was visible in the sky during the painfully hot days of the end of summer. A later writer described the ancients as believing that these were days when "the sea boiled, the wine turned sour, dogs grew mad, and all other creatures became languid; causing to man, among other diseases, burning fevers, hysterics, and phrensies" (John Brady, *Clavis Calendaria*, 1813).

After being unconscious for three hours on my "birthday," it took three full days for me to feel reconnected to the world. On April 14, I finally fully woke up. The haze of the last few days was gone. I talked to a few friends on the phone before starting to feel nauseated. A nurse gave me medication to help control the nausea, and I immediately fell asleep. This wasn't a dozing sort of nap—I was knocked out! Yet another drug on the "do not give" list.

When I finally awakened from my stupor, I was wiped out and aware that the lucidity I had experienced that morning had been just a small window that was now shut. I dozed off and on for the rest of the afternoon, waking sporadically with general pain and discomfort. How long would this last? No one could tell me. I was back to a waiting game, this time for the transplanted cells to take hold and begin producing my new immune system. These dog days would continue until engraftment, the point when new white cells could be detected swimming in my blood, indicating the stem cells are working.

Until then, I was confined to the sterile part of the eighth floor. This was my bubble. I was not allowed any visitors other than my caregivers, and they had to wash up and "gown up" before they entered my room. At the end of the day, my mom reminded me I needed to walk to aid my recovery. Eventually, the doctors wanted me walking the halls three times a day, but today was my first attempt at leaving my room without a wheelchair. The staff were quite nervous about me falling, so they fitted me with a walking gait belt. This made me feel more secure. A strong nurse could hold on to the back of the belt and ensure I didn't fall. I left the room with great trepidation, but I had an entourage to back me up: my mom, the nurse I normally saw in my room, and a strong, cute male nurse holding me up. One lap around the reception area was as far as I could go. This was not something a marathoner would usually aspire to, but it was all I had in me.

☙ • ☙ • ☙

Day 5: You Never Know What Is Going to Happen
Journal entry by Mike — 4/16/2014

Rachel is having a better day than she has had for some time. Her speech and cognition are increasingly better, recovering from the seizure she had as a result of the stem cell infusion on Day 0.

This is Mike writing, which leads to the theme for this post. It seems one of the lessons of this whole process is that you really don't know what is going to happen next. Yesterday morning I was carrying on with home duties. Got Noah off to school, did some laundry, got Hannah working on another Lego city, etc. Then Margaret called. She was starting to feel the first effects of a cold and had to leave the hospital so she would not infect Rachel. By noon, I had a flight to Seattle and my sister-in-law Janice was on her way up to Blue River from Eugene to watch the kids.

Rachel is feeling pretty good, or as she just said, "Today is tolerable." She has a lot of pain in her mouth and throat.

Apparently the mucus cells are fast growing and heavily affected by the chemo. Her strength is up to the point that she has twice walked a few circuits of the ward, and she has been awake for more than half the day. She has had one transfusion of platelets and another of packed red cells and managed to get down almost half a cup of applesauce. Talking with the doctor, I expect this will be temporary. She will start feeling worse for the next five days or so, until engraftment.

This morning I noticed Rachel's hands. Over the past year she had developed a tremor in both hands from the MS. She also has had tremendous pain. Today I noticed the tremor is almost entirely gone, and she is reporting no MS pain. I hope that is the beginning sign of healing.

Up to this point my caretakers had been sleeping in my room for my comfort. To be honest, I was scared to be alone at night, but I knew it wasn't sustainable. The recliner bed that was provided for them to sleep on was not comfortable, and my father would not have been able to sleep well even if there had been a decent bed. Several times a night a nurse came in to change bags, look at dressings, and take vitals. My dad was so nervous about my lack of an immune system at this point that he would get up to supervise the nurses' hand-washing. He even questioned one or two of them when he thought it hadn't been done well enough. After a few nights, he finally had enough. He told me he needed to sleep in the hotel room from here on out. "I am just not getting enough sleep," he said. "I can be of more help to you if I can be alert and on guard during the day and let the nursing staff take care of you at night."

The Romans didn't mention mucositis when they discussed dog days centuries ago, but that's what mine had in store for me. Mucositis is an inflammation of the mouth and throat that, in my case, was caused by chemotherapy. It was totally expected, but that didn't make it any less painful. Swallowing became so difficult that I had to get my fluids and nutrition, along with all my medication, through an IV. Dad was right about that half a cup of applesauce—it was the last food I swallowed for several days.

I experienced the worst of the mucositis the first night I was in the hospital alone. After a routine check in the middle of the night, I dozed off when the nurse left. But almost immediately I awoke in extreme pain. It felt as if I had swallowed a dozen razor blades. I pushed the nurse call button. Before she got there, I became nauseated and threw up. The nurse was just walking in when I stopped puking and looked into the pink plastic basin I was holding. I was looking at something out of a horror movie. It was not normal vomit or even bile, but bloody chunks of tissue. When I looked closer, I saw a two-inch-long blood-covered fleshy tube of some sort. "I think you should come take a look at this," I told the nurse in a panic-stricken voice. She calmly picked up the bin and said, "Yes, this happens. Don't worry, it's totally normal."

She walked across the room and picked up a phone. She tried to speak softly, but I could hear her. "I think you

need to check this out, Doctor. I'll get it there right away."
Then she picked up the basin and hurried out the door. This
did not reassure me. Her whispered conversation made it
clear this was not, in fact, normal. I called my dad to tell
him what had happened, hoping he might come back to the
hospital. The poor guy was just too tired. He assured me the
nurses could handle it and told me he would come straight
to the hospital when he woke up.

I tried to go back to sleep, but I was too anxious. My
dad wasn't coming, and the nurse had rushed off to show a
doctor whatever had just come out of my stomach. Before
I was able to muster up a full panic, the nurse reappeared.
The doctor had examined the tissue and confirmed it was
nothing to worry about. It was the lining to my esophagus.
Gagging it up like that would probably make swallowing
even more painful for a while, but it was just the effects of
the chemotherapy.

A couple of days after the esophagus incident, I had
another unexpected medical problem. During a routine
echocardiogram, doctors detected a blood clot. The clot was
attached to the wall of my heart in the right atrium, next
to the Hickman line. This was not something they could
fix right away; dislodging the clot could cause a pulmonary
embolism. The only course of action was to give me heparin
(a blood thinner) to dissolve the clot. Before they could
start, however, my platelet count had to rise. I was already
being pumped full of antibiotics, antifungals, morphine,
Benadryl, nutritional agents, and more medications I can't

even remember. Now, on top of everything else, I was receiving blood transfusions.

With the many tubes hooked up to me 24/7, I felt like a spider in the middle of a web. I was continually being reminded to be careful when I got up. I was supposed to ask for help, even to walk into the bathroom, but I was obstinate and refused to call a nurse each time. I felt totally capable of calmly and carefully walking into the bathroom holding on to my IV pole. Once when my father observed my solo trip back and forth, he reported that he saw me moving like a wild person, with my arms flailing around in fast-forward. He too emphasized that I needed to call a nurse when I wanted to move around my room.

The next day I had a rare moment in my room alone. Dad was out for a walk, and there were no nurses, doctors, or orderlies in sight. This never happened. In spite of the warnings and the description of my erratic movements, I took the opportunity to change my clothes by myself. I had been unable to do simple self-care tasks by myself for days. For God's sake, I just wanted to change my underwear in private! It felt wonderful to walk across the room freely and pick out a clean outfit for myself. I knew I had to be quick, because someone could walk in at any time. I did not want to be chastised for this small show of independence.

I needed to figure out how to change while remaining hooked up to the equipment that followed me everywhere. Moving as fast as I could, I managed to put on fresh clothes before anyone returned. I was proud of myself for managing all of this without a problem. But when I turned around, the floor of my room looked as if someone had just slaughtered an animal on it. I did a quick self-assessment. I felt no new pain, so I didn't think I had hurt myself, but the crimson pool on the floor was getting steadily larger.

I hit the emergency button to call a nurse for help. As I waited, I noticed that my Hickman line was no longer connected to anything. I must have severed it while I was changing. I panicked and rushed to get back to the bed so it would not look as if I had caused the bloodbath. But when the nurse arrived it was pretty obvious what had happened. She calmly informed me that I was now on lockdown. From that point on I had an alarm on my bed that alerted the nurses' station every time I got up. I had really screwed myself. I had been so eager to embrace a moment of privacy and freedom that now I had neither.

☉ • ☉ • ☉

The dog days weren't all bad, however. Even though my throat felt excruciatingly raw, I noticed that I was not feeling the intense neuropathic pain that had plagued me daily for the past five years. My father also noticed that the tremor I had developed in both hands was almost entirely gone.

Another piece of good news came when the search for neutrophils in my blood finally yielded positive numbers. Neutrophils are short-lived, general-purpose white blood cells that are the accepted indicator that stem cells have established themselves and are functioning normally. In the beginning, the number was extremely low, but I was assured that once this number started to climb, my pain and fatigue would subside. Every new white blood cell that appeared represented a baby step toward leaving the hospital.

I even had a moment during the dog days when I was able to forget my pain and feel truly happy. Being away from Josh so much over the last few months had been very difficult. Seeing him now during my confinement to the sterile unit lifted my spirits. One day, after he greeted me and settled in, he reached for his bag. Then he got down on one knee. He held out a little black box and said, "Rachel, with these new stem cells, will you still be my wife?"

I was floored. I had known he would replace my wedding ring someday, but given everything we were going through, I assumed it wouldn't be a priority for a long time. I was overjoyed.

The ring was beautiful. He had even paired it with a ten-year anniversary band to honor all we had been through in our marriage. In that moment, I wasn't a patient. I wasn't handicapped. I wasn't a specimen to be poked, prodded, and studied. I was a beautiful beloved woman and wife.

14

NEW LEASE ON LIFE

Two weeks after the transplant, I was finally eating on my own. I still experienced pain when I swallowed Cream of Wheat, but at least I could swallow.

The Gold Team began preparing me for my discharge. They detached my tubes, as I was now able to take medication orally. Everyone was encouraged that I was doing so well, but I was scared. It felt too soon. Was I ready to leave the hospital? How could they be sure I would be all right? Help was steps away while I was in the hospital, not blocks. The building had become a security blanket for me. I didn't want to leave.

But, expect the unexpected. Saturday I went to sleep nervous about leaving; Sunday I awoke with a severe rash covering my body. I had engraftment syndrome, which occurs in some patients at the time of neutrophil recovery following HSCT. Aside from the rash and fever, the pain was back as well. All of my MS symptoms were manifesting themselves with a vengeance. Once again the nurse began hanging fluids on the IV pole. The pain medication was back as well as intravenous steroids to combat the syndrome. Engraftment syndrome can lead to liver and renal dysfunction, so a different antiviral drip was now being administered, one that was less damaging to the liver.

A day later, the engraftment syndrome was under control and my blood counts continued to grow. I was back on oral pain meds and the team gave me the option to leave that afternoon. We began the process of packing up. I would leave with only one necessary infusion, the antiviral drip; otherwise I was tube free, except for the Hickman line in my chest.

By 8:00 p.m. on Day 17, my mom and I were back in the hotel room with our feet up, watching TV. Just like that, my hospital stay was over.

☺•☺•☺

The hesitation and fear I felt about leaving SCCA disappeared after one night of normalcy back at the hotel. I was amazed how much better this change of scenery made me feel. Looking back, my fear and hesitation of the preceding days seemed foolish. Who doesn't want to be out of the hospital? I couldn't tell if my good mood was a result of actually feeling better or if I was just that happy to be back out in the world. But it didn't matter. I couldn't remember the last time I had felt so normal. I even got inspired to dress up and put on makeup. Bald or not, I wanted to look my best. After all, I was a new person, with a future now. I wanted to show the world I was here to stay.

Dr. Georges and the rest of the Gold Team had emphasized from the beginning that the goal of my treatment was to stop the progression of my MS; it would be years before I would know to what extent my brain would heal or even if it would heal at all. But in the days after I left the hospital, I even got on the treadmill in the hotel gym. After being utterly drained and miserable for so long, it is impossible to describe how it felt to be able to walk for twenty consecutive minutes. Prior to treatment, I had almost completely given up on my future. Now I believed I would have a life again—I was not merely surviving. After all I had been through, the feeling of hope was beyond amazing. I felt as if a thousand-pound weight had been lifted from my shoulders and my soul.

Even in my euphoria, I knew I couldn't trust this invincible feeling to last long. I was still extremely vulnerable to infection. This meant avoiding crowds, drinking only boiled or bottled water, not eating certain foods, and making sure the foods I did eat were thoroughly cleaned and cooked. I was still taking antibiotics, antifungals, and antivirals. I also had to be monitored carefully by my team at SCCA to make sure my blood counts remained within the target range and to check for two common viruses that often show up at this stage in recovery. And, in the back of my mind, I knew my "I'm doing so great!" assessment was skewed by how terrible I had felt before and during the treatment. As my father pointed out, when someone who used to run twenty-six miles rejoices at being able to walk up a flight of stairs, that person isn't exactly *healthy*. But I was getting better.

One morning, I woke up and decided to test my balance. A year ago, during the approval process for the Chicago program, I had been unable to walk on my heels, stand on one foot, or touch my nose with my eyes closed. I remember crying when I realized my disability was so clearly on display. So there in my Seattle hotel room, I spread my arms, lifted my right foot to my left knee, and stood like that for a few seconds. Then I switched and did the same with my left foot. Once both feet were back on the ground, I lifted my toes, balanced on my heels, and walked across the room. Finally, I closed my eyes and touched my nose. My father was the only witness. I couldn't believe it, and neither could he. I can't be sure, but I think he had tears in his eyes.

The neurologist, Dr. Bowen, was just as surprised as my father that I was able to balance so well. When I went in for a checkup a few weeks after my discharge, he said that transplant patients usually don't see much improvement until the two-month mark. We agreed my improvements might seem more noticeable because I had been in such bad shape when I arrived. My speech was still slightly slurred and had been ever since I had lost consciousness during the transplant. He said this would likely go away with time. My body, he explained, was working so hard rebuilding my immune system that it didn't have much energy left over to work on my brain right now.

The weeks after my discharge afforded me the opportunity to recognize and reflect on how many people had rallied around me and my recovery. My parents had been my rotating caretakers throughout the entire treatment process and when they weren't with me they were taking care of Noah and Hannah at their house in Blue River. One of Josh's sisters and her family were taking care of Marin in Lincoln City on the coast of Oregon. His other sister spent countless hours driving Marin from Lincoln City to Vancouver so she could visit Josh. Josh continued working full time in Portland while burning up the highways every weekend driving to Blue River, Lincoln City, and Seattle and helping to make arrangements for my care after Seattle. Then there were the countless friends and cousins who had come to Seattle to cheer me on, aunts who had pinch-hit with the kids while my parents were swapping out their posts, other relatives who had helped with errands large and small, and all the sweet, thoughtful people who had sent cards and care packages. People's capacity for kindness is astonishing.

☺ • ☺ • ☺

Finally, on Friday, May 30, I got permission to leave Seattle. My mom and I packed up the car and checked out of the hotel that morning in anticipation that the Gold

Team would find my blood viral levels stable enough for me to go home. By the time the nurses administered all the tests, it was 1:00 p.m. It took another three and a half hours to round up all the pharmaceuticals and supplies, and we didn't get on the freeway until 4:30. With traffic and a stop for dinner, we arrived in Blue River slightly after midnight. We were, as my mother put it, "a couple of horses headed to the barn."

Josh and Marin had arrived in Blue River earlier that day to join my dad and Hannah and Noah, and we spent an amazing weekend together as a family. The kids were overjoyed to have both parents together again. Marin had just two weeks left to finish up the school year in Lincoln City. After that she would move down for a Blue River summer. Josh would drive down from Vancouver to visit us on the weekends.

Being with my children again, especially now that I wasn't in constant pain, was bliss. But the transition had its challenges. The last few weeks of my life in Seattle had been calm and simple. I could sleep when and for as long as I needed to. In Blue River there was considerably more activity, and children naturally require a lot of energy from the adults around them. I was also transitioning from super-strong steroids to weaker ones, which diminished my energy level. But none of that mattered. I was with my family; I was home.

One beautiful day about a week after my arrival in Blue River, I took a walk in the woods with my father.

Feeling the sun on my face and smelling the Douglas firs, I was profoundly struck by how much we humans take for granted. I was completely overwhelmed with gratitude; I was walking on clouds. In that moment, I believe God officially delivered to me my new lease on life.

15

THE ME I AM NOW

Before my encounter with Suzie in the school parking lot, before I sought acceptance into a stem cell transplant program, I thought my journey on Earth was near its end. But I was wrong. Arriving in Seattle on February 24, 2014, changed the trajectory of my life's story. Leaving Seattle three months later ended the old chapter.

But I did not write this book just to tell the story of my transplant. I want my journey to benefit others. I want my experience to serve as an inspiration, a tool, a guide for anyone who might connect with it. This is not a story only about a woman with multiple sclerosis; it is about the medical community and the constant progress being made in finding treatments and cures for many diseases. It is about surviving even the most harrowing circumstances. And it is about how human beings are resilient and kind and strong. "One more step" and hope brought me through to the other side of my disease, but my story doesn't end there. My recovery began a whole new chapter.

I cannot report the full extent of my recovery yet, as I am only four years out; some people in the medical field think that total recovery from HSCT can take up to eight years. It took me roughly two years to feel hopeful that I might live a relatively normal life again. After three years I had physically recovered from the chemotherapy, but the brain damage that MS had caused will always be there. I feel compelled to gift readers with the knowledge of all the mistakes I made during those years as I learned what it really takes to recover from a procedure as traumatic to the body as a stem cell transplant. Here are some my biggest takeaways and most revealing stories from my recovery.

Support System: Got to Have One

My new lease on life would not have been possible without support from my family and friends. I am blessed to have parents who had the resources—emotional, practical, and financial—to be able to help me and my family at every step of my journey. I also have a husband who was my tireless advocate when bureaucracy threatened to derail my treatment plan. I know not everyone has what I have, but for anyone who is considering a transplant, I would urge you to identify the people in your life you can depend on and don't be afraid to ask them for help.

Leaving Seattle was the beginning of a new chapter for my support team as well; everything in our lives was about to change. While I was recovering in the weeks immediately following my transplant, Josh and I decided to sell our house in Vancouver, Washington, and buy a house in Gilbert, Arizona. This seems like a crazy thing to do, but it made sense at the time. Josh was, as always, looking ahead and had read up on all of the possible negative factors for someone recovering from a stem cell transplant. It turned out that we were living in one of the worst areas of the United States for fighting off infection. The Pacific Northwest is moist and mold grows easily there. Arizona, in contrast, is dry. Josh had visited his best friend in Gilbert. (Don't forget that caretakers need an occasional break!) While there, he discovered that the housing development his friend lived in was still growing, and he saw a model home that had all of the features we wanted for our next house. Most importantly, it was a single-level home. The stairs in our old house had become my nemesis, and we still had no idea how well I would recover. We wanted a house I could move through with as little difficulty as possible; having a brand-new house without years of built-up dirt and bad memories was a bonus.

When Josh brought up the idea of moving to Arizona, I told him he was out of his mind. I was still very limited in what I could do in a day; I knew there was no way I could possibly handle packing and moving. My top priority was to recover, and I didn't need any additional stress slowing that down. But Josh said he would do everything himself, and—after lots of discussion on why he thought the move was a good idea—I agreed. I was skeptical that he could do everything himself, but over the last few years I had learned to trust Josh when it came to making decisions and taking care of things. He had proven that he could make almost anything happen, so I put my faith in him. And he did it. By the time I left the hospital in Seattle, all of our belongings were in storage.

My support team and I decided that a summer near my parents would be a good start to my recovery. No one thought I was ready to resume full responsibility of three children and a household. Fortunately, the property next to my parents' is a vacation home. The owner was open to letting us rent his house for the months we needed. It was an ideal situation: the rental was fully furnished, I had no possessions to worry about, and anything I needed I could borrow from my parents. The week before I left Seattle, my parents asked their friends for help to prepare the house so my kids and I could move in. Josh would live at my sister's house in Portland to be close to work during the week and then stay with us on the weekends.

It took a group of eight adults three full days to sterilize the house so it was safe for me and my nonexistent immune system to live in. My parents sterilized their own house as well, and my father blazed a trail across the small wooded area between the two properties to provide an easy shortcut.

Over the next few months while I was living next to my parents, Josh sold our home in Vancouver. We were ready to move to Arizona as soon as our new house was built. On top of that he convinced his company to allow him to work from Arizona most of the time with flights to Portland every few weeks. We were starting over again, in a new place and—finally—together.

Wait and See: Patience Is Key

While I lived at the rental next to my parents, I was getting better day by day, but I was still having cognitive deficits and slurred speech. The worst part was that if I tried to do anything that involved more than one task at a time I became overwhelmed and extremely emotional, which made it even harder for my mind to put thoughts together. It felt as if my brain would completely shut down except for nonsensical thoughts. Arbitrary words ran through my mind. These words seemed like they might be thoughts if I could just put them together in the right order, but I couldn't grab onto them. This worried me greatly. Was this the new normal for me?

Then there was the forgetfulness. Every Tuesday morning I filled my pill dispenser for the week. Believe me, it was quite a task. I still had many pills to take several times a day. One particular Tuesday when I set up my weekly regimen, I realized I was missing the prescription I had picked up from the pharmacy the previous day. This sent me into a complete panic. What was I going to do without the pills I needed?

After searching my purse, my house, and then my parents' house without result, I asked for their assistance.

They retraced my steps after I had arrived home with the prescriptions. I just could not remember the actions of the day before. Eventually this led me to the trash. Apparently, when emptying out the car on coming home, I had thrown away the white pharmacy bag. I was always surprised, and depressed, by experiences like this that made me feel as if my brain had turned into mush. In many ways, the mental recovery was harder than the physical recovery for me. I hated the terrible "cog fog." Thankfully, it did eventually improve, but it took the better part of three years.

It wasn't just the slow return of my mental function that taught me the value of patience, as this next story reveals. About a hundred days after my transplant, I woke up with a terrible pain in my chest. It had always been sore from the Hickman line loosely dangling from the gruesome hole near my sternum, but this was a deeper pain. Was it coming from inside my heart? As far as I knew, the clot my medical team had discovered was still there. I decided I had to consult my parents right away, and they agreed I should not take this lightly. We waited for twenty or thirty minutes to confirm it wasn't a fleeting ache. Then I called the post-transplant triage nurse line in Seattle, which led to my father driving me to the ER an hour away.

We reached the hospital in the early afternoon and didn't leave until the following morning. When we finally got the X-ray taken and read, it revealed that my blood clot was completely gone. The Hickman line hadn't been used in weeks, but the fear that removing it could dislodge the clot had been preventing the elimination of this useless apparatus. Now it could be removed!

I expected the removal to require another surgical procedure, since that was how it had been put in. I was wrong. A young man in scrubs entered the room my father and I had been moved to. "You must be the doctor," I said. "Nope, I'm a technician," he responded. Before I could ask how he would remove the line, he leaned over and pulled it out in one smooth movement. It was not the not a big deal I was expecting. Just like that, the tube was gone. We never did find out what had caused the chest pain, but it too was gone.

Since the discovery of the blood clot, I had been on a blood thinner called heparin. Twice a day I gave myself shots. The heparin caused severe bruising whenever I bumped into something, and the Hickman line had to be flushed daily. Having that tube hanging from my chest had also been a visible sign of my illness. Now it was gone, along with the medication I no longer needed. I could shower normally, I could run, I could sleep on my stomach without fear, and—best of all—I could let my children crawl on me.

The Hickman line had been a part of me for so long I had stopped imagining what life would be like without it. Having it removed made me realize that—as slowly as it was happening—I *was* getting better. I wasn't always the most patient patient, but this experience bolstered my faith that things were moving in the right direction.

Worry and Fear: They're a Waste of Time

There was always the underlying fear that the HSCT hadn't worked for me. One night I took a bath and thought my leg was numb. It turned out it wasn't; the leg felt normal again after a minute or two. But the fear of this unknown was something I lived with on a daily basis, and I didn't feel that I could tell anyone about it. It felt unfair to burden the people who had seen me through this ordeal with the idea that it might not have worked. I tried to feel only gratitude that I had had this chance for a cure, but it was hard not to worry that I would be one of the 15 percent who continued to regress after a transplant.

I also didn't want to waste the days when I *was* feeling better worrying about my speech and cognition problems. I tried to focus on the fact that I was improving physically, but even that became a worry. Why hadn't I gotten sick yet? People usually get very sick post transplant after they leave the safety of the hospital, and I had not. My stack of worries was growing.

I don't know if it was the contrast with how terrible I had felt before the transplant and the misery of the transplant itself, but feeling physically well was nice. It was so nice that I made the mistake of overdoing it. A lot. The fact that I was trying to get stronger with Pilates and yoga just three months post transplant was insanity. After those hour-long workouts I had days where I never got out of bed because I was too fatigued to do anything. It was a vicious cycle.

A contributing factor to this was that I was continuing to take steroids for much longer than my doctors in Seattle recommended. The doctor I was seeing locally for post-transplant care didn't read or didn't follow my discharge instructions, which is probably why I felt as if I could work out when I should have been resting. I was once again reminded that you can't trust doctors to do everything correctly. *You have to be cognizant of your own care.*

Although I was physically more comfortable except for the fatigue, I felt unsettled. I was constantly on guard, waiting . . . but for what? Part of it was obvious: I was waiting to be completely healed, but that was way down the road. Something else was making me restless. Three months post transplant, that unknown something hit me.

I had my first "bad day." I was feeling even more fatigued than usual, and my limbs felt as if they each weighed a hundred pounds. I spent the entire day in my bathrobe at my parents' house so I could let go of all responsibilities.

The blessing that came with that bad day was the knowledge that I could handle it. I let go of being scared; I didn't have to worry, because I knew I would feel better tomorrow. Part of the despair of my days prior to treatment was not knowing if there would ever be an end to the horrific pain. But at this point in my recovery, I finally knew it was just for one day. And sure, it might be more than one, but I knew it would end.

More good news came shortly after my epiphany: my hair was finally growing in. It was similar to baby chick fuzz, but it was filling in enough that I no longer looked as if I had hair plugs. One less thing to worry about—I would not be bald forever!

Despite these small signs of returning normalcy, I still spent a lot of time after the transplant feeling bad about my appearance. I had gained a lot of weight and, even with the fuzz, I was pretty much bald. I looked pale and sick and I no longer recognized myself. The daily blow to my confidence when I looked in the mirror was a constant struggle; I wasted a lot of time being unhappy with my appearance. In retrospect, I wish I hadn't worried about it. How a person looks when they're sick should not be a concern. And it turned out, three years later I looked like myself again. My suggestion is to not look in the mirror at all for the first year post transplant!

Something I started getting better at during this time was accepting myself flaws and all. This is good advice for life in general, not just for recovery, but it took recovery for me to see it clearly. I noticed right away that the better I got at accepting my current state, the less I worried and the happier I was. I have always had an illusion that I can be perfect. That is just not possible, and this journey of recovery has made this even more obvious to me.

Settle In: This Is Real Life

As the move to Arizona grew closer, I became increasingly nervous. My brain was still not working well, and I often felt overwhelmed. Even though most of our belongings were packed up, I was in a quagmire when it came to keeping track of the dates for the phases of the move. When did I need to pack up our clothes and personal items? When was the last day of school for my kids? What was the deadline for enrolling them in their new school? Where would I get the medical follow-up I needed? How would I manage to drive over a thousand miles from Oregon to Arizona? What had lived as an abstract thought in my mind was starting to feel very, very real.

I needed to find solutions to help me make it through this stressful time. One was simply printing out a calendar where I could write deadlines and keep track of the progress needed for the move. A visual aid was extremely helpful. Then I contacted a good friend to see if she would be willing to take that long drive with me, three kids, one beagle, and two cats. When she agreed to make the trip with me, I was greatly relieved.

Our departure date from Oregon finally arrived. In early December, 239 days post transplant, my car was loaded. The kids and I bundled in with hands full of homemade cinnamon rolls, and I left my parents' nest—again—for our new life in Arizona.

Now I was in a new reality without the backup I'd had for months. Everything was up to me: unpacking our belongings, helping the kids adjust to their new school, and managing my recovery. I reflected on the odd fact that I had felt better and stronger right out of treatment. Now that energy had dwindled. Just a few minutes of activity led to more time on the couch.

Whenever I started feeling discouraged about my limits, I deliberately reflected on how much better I was than just one year earlier. Whenever I felt sorry for myself or as if I wasn't doing enough, I made the comparison. This made the guilt and sorrow go away and helped me learn to accept my limitations and continue to heal. Since I had entered the Seattle study, the waiting times for the programs performing HSCT for multiple sclerosis had grown to two years or more. I honestly don't think I would have made it two more years. I had been lucky.

It was frustrating how many events I couldn't attend because there was too much risk of getting sick with just a common cold. I had moved to a new region with new germs that my children would bring home on a regular basis. And every cold I got turned into a sinus infection.

So here I was, without the backup of my parents living next door, facing a string of illnesses. Along with the colds, I fell ill with swine flu. Following that I woke up one morning with severe pain around my torso. I had shingles. My new doctor at the Scottsdale Mayo Clinic told me it was one of the worst cases she'd ever seen. I later learned that getting shingles is fairly common among HSCT patients. I'm not going to lie; the combination of constant illnesses and lack of support was very hard for me. But I knew I needed to trust the recovery process and roll with the punches. This was my real life. I had fought hard for it and I was lucky to have it—shingles and all.

Don't Overdo It: Feed Them Hot Dogs

After everything settled down in the new house and most of the unpacking was done, I gained confidence that I was going to be able to take care of my family on my own. I decided to celebrate my newfound assurance by cooking a nice dinner. It was a disaster. I made fried pork chops, and when I threw the first chop into the oil-filled frying pan, it splashed back on me, throwing globs of boiling-hot grease-soaked flour onto my neck. Instead of eating a nice dinner, my family went to the ER.

Several hours and hundreds of dollars later, I was headed home with yet another bandage I had to change daily and more scars to look forward to.

The next day, Josh gave me a much-needed gift. I asked him what he thought I should do that day, and he practically shouted the answer at me: "Nothing! I need you to recover, and every time you do something you hurt yourself. Please," he pleaded with me, "just sit there."

He was right. What he and the kids needed from me was for me to be there physically and mentally. They didn't need fancy dinners or Pinterest-worthy homemade birthday cakes. They needed connection and companionship and love. And I needed to conserve my energy to be able to give them those things.

The New Normal:
Two Steps Forward, One Step Back

After I left Seattle, people naturally asked how I was doing. Usually I responded with a resounding "Great!" But the truth was, I was not great, and I may never be great on a daily basis again.

When I first talked to my hematologist about my difficulties keeping up with the kids or working out for an hour or how hard life was in general, I got the reality check I needed. She laughed at me. "Raising three kids is hard on anyone," she said kindly, and she reminded me that some people never fully recover from a stem cell transplant. My maximum recovery might take five to eight years, and even then it wouldn't be unusual to regain only 80 percent of the strength and endurance I had had previously. That is the reality. When I asked her about exercise, she advised me to walk, and no more than fifteen minutes at a time in the beginning. I was starting from zero, and my body would feel awkward for a while.

The purpose of HSCT for multiple sclerosis is to stop further progression. Anything more than that is a bonus. This knowledge brought me to tears at times. I had envisioned being able to run miles again, to keep up with everyone else and do fun activities with my kids. I could not. I got too fatigued, and the more I fought it, the longer I would be fatigued.

As hard as it was, I did eventually begin listening more closely to my body and giving myself a break emotionally for not always pushing to do more. Being gentle with myself wasn't my natural instinct, but I slowly learned to focus more on gratitude for the gains I had made than on frustration over the ones I had not.

For the first year, I had pain in my body every morning when I woke up. I'll never know if it was nerve damage from MS or a result of the havoc chemotherapy had wreaked on my body, but it was there every morning. During this time there were days I stayed in bed all day. Then, gradually, the morning pain decreased and eventually vanished altogether.

At two years post transplant, I often had energy for several days of activity in a row instead of just one. I started to lose weight, and my normal figure was returning. I developed a daily routine of making my kids breakfast and sack lunches in the morning and a family dinner at night without feeling overwhelmed. I often napped in the afternoon and certainly was ready for bed early—sometimes earlier than my kids.

At three years, my hair had completely grown back, and I had never more appreciated being able to pull it back into a ponytail. The three-year mark was also when I started feeling more normal exercising. I was able to jog for intervals on my walks, and it felt natural again.

Now at four years out, I have found my new normal. I can move easily most of the time, and the morning pain is gone. My brain fog has mostly subsided, though it still surprises me sometimes. The slurred speech makes an appearance only when I am not rested, and I am finally comfortable for most of the day.

Was It Worth It:
Hell Yes!

A question many people ask after they've heard I've had HSCT is "Was it worth it?" For people with MS, I always tell them that I cannot know if it would be worth it for them. It depends on each person's personal situation. When I faced this groundbreaking treatment and all the accompanying risk factors, I had no other option. I was barely living, so it didn't matter if I died. At least the pain would stop. I know that sounds extreme, but so was my situation.

I was in such dire straits before the transplant that I could not take care of my children. I could not even take care of myself. I rarely left my bed. I could not cross a room without aid. I thought—and my father told me he had this thought as well—that if the disease didn't kill me, I would eventually have to take my own life, given the amount of horrific neuropathic pain I experienced constantly.

So for me, it was not a choice. It was a necessity so that I could have a chance to go on being a mother to the three precious children I had brought into this world. I owed it to them.

And yet there have been many times since my HSCT when I've asked myself the same question: "Was it worth it?"

Admittedly, there were weeks on end during which I was very ill and feared I would never get better. On the days when I would lie in bed all day, I felt incredibly lonely and unproductive. On those days I asked myself, "Was it worth it?" and I wasn't sure.

I am now sure that it *was* worth it! And not just because I'm out of bed every day and cooking for my family again. I am one of a handful of people who know what it is to face death. I have changed as a person. My faith is stronger. My compassion for myself and others has deepened. I am always grateful now, even in the face of hardship.

I may never work outside my home again. I know I will never run another marathon or even a 10K. But I have figured out how to live my life. And if you're navigating your own MS journey, don't ever give up. I am living proof that miracles do happen.

ACKNOWLEDGMENTS

My greatest thanks go to my children, Marin, Noah, and Hannah, for giving me the reason to go on when I didn't think I could. I thank my husband, Josh, for making this treatment possible, for getting me through it, for being by my side as I recovered, and for his patience and his support of my determination to tell my story. I thank both of my parents, Margaret and Mike Godfrey, for their immeasurable support of me and my family throughout the transplant and throughout the process of writing this book so I can offer support to others.

Many people helped get me through the tough times, first before I knew of a treatment for MS, and then while I waited to see if the treatment would be a reality for me. Thanks go to my church family, who brought meals to my home and sent me off to my treatment in Seattle with a huge gathering of well-wishers. I am also thankful for my coworkers, who did their best to keep me working as long as I could. My extended family came to my rescue numerous times, taking me and my children in for days until I could function again. Once I was in treatment, family members welcomed my children into their homes for the duration of my hospital stay. I don't think I could have had a more ideal support system to get me through this period of my life.

I thank Adrienne van der Valk both for seeing the importance of this book from the beginning and for helping me bring it to life. Adrienne, my mother, and I spent years emailing and telephoning back and forth editing and improving the writing and storytelling. Russell Estes gave his skills to the design of the book. Anna Embree deserves huge thanks for her professional editing. I am extremely grateful for the lengths she went to to truly understand every part of my story and to make sure the final version stayed true both to what happened and to my feelings about it. Finally, I thank Dr. Janice Rutherford for the final edit.

I also want to thank the first readers who helped Enduring the Cure become its very best: Dr. Janice Rutherford, Suzanne van der Valk, Joe Ebin, Will Pollard, Mike Godfrey, and Chris Walker.

GLOSSARY

A-B-C drugs (Avonex, Betaseron, and Copaxone)

The first disease-modifying therapy for MS, these drugs became available in the 1990s, before Rachel was diagnosed. Copaxone is injected daily and sometimes has a small site reaction similar to a bee sting. Betaseron is injected every other day and creates a burning feeling while it enters the body. Avonex is a weekly injection that results in flu-like symptoms for one or two days. Rachel tried all three of these in her efforts to slow the progression of her MS, with no success.

anti-thymocyte globulin (ATG)

Antibodies used to kill human T-cells. ATG is created by injecting human T-cells into rabbits or horses. The animals' immune systems create antibodies that are then harvested to give back to humans. In Rachel's case, ATG was used to destroy any of her T-cells that remained after chemotherapy, because these old T-cells harbored the memory that caused them to start an immune reaction to myelin. It is not uncommon to have an adverse reaction to ATG; Rachel had a particularly severe reaction.

aphaeresis

The procedure of removing blood from a patient, separating out one component (such as stem cells), and returning the remainder to the patient. Rachel's stem cells were removed by aphaeresis and stored until their reintroduction post-BEAM.

Ativan

A trade name for the drug lorazepam, a sedative used to treat anxiety. This was the preferred drug for treating Rachel's anxiety attacks during her time in Seattle.

atrium

Either of the two upper chambers of the heart. Rachel developed a blood clot in her right atrium.

autologous hematopoietic stem cell transplant (HSCT)

A treatment that uses chemotherapy to destroy a malfunctioning immune system and then regenerates it using new stem cells from the same individual. During HSCT, the immune system is "reset." Rachel first heard about HSCT in the parking lot of her kids' school.

BEAM

A high-dose chemotherapy named after the initials of the drugs used: BiCNU (carmustine), etoposide, Ara-C (cytarabine), and melphalan. BEAM is usually given before a stem cell transplant to destroy fast-growing cells in the body, including the immune system. Rachel was admitted to the hospital to receive BEAM treatment.

Bell's palsy

A condition that weakens or paralyzes the muscles on one side of a person's face and causes it to droop on that side. The condition often comes on quickly and is caused by a variety of factors, including nerve inflammation. Rachel experienced Bell's palsy prior to being diagnosed with MS.

birthday

The day an HSCT patient gets their new stem cells and begins growing a new immune system. Rachel's "birthday" is April 11, 2014.

black hole

An area in the brain that appears black on an MRI image due to severe loss of myelin and underlying axons. A black hole indicates permanent brain damage, and black holes correlate strongly with disability levels. Rachel has three black holes.

CT (computed tomography) scan

An X-ray process for producing cross-sectional images or "slices" of the body or brain. After Rachel lost consciousness on her "birthday," the medical staff used a CT scan to rule out a brain bleed.

cure

This is the trickiest word to define in this book. *Cure* is the accepted medical term for when a person shows no symptoms of a disease they had previously and remains symptom free for an arbitrary period of time (often five years). This is a word that Rachel uses in her book; however, she still has symptoms from the previous MS damage to her body. Thanks to HSCT, any further MS damage is halted. Rachel views this as a cure.

Cytoxan

A brand name for cytophosphane, a mild form of chemotherapy used to stop cell growth. It is also used to mobilize stem cells to move from the bone marrow into the bloodstream. Rachel used Cytoxan to mobilize her stem cells and suppress her immune system because she had an active MS exacerbation when she began her HSCT treatment.

dimethyl sulfoxide (DMSO)

A clear odorless liquid commonly used as a solvent. When stem cells are frozen after collection, DMSO is used to help preserve the harvested cells. DMSO is thought to be involved in Rachel's loss of consciousness on her "birthday."

disease-modifying therapy (DMT)

Drugs that can reduce the number and severity of MS relapses. They can also slow the MS damage that builds up over time. Rachel tried every DMT available to her at the time, but her decline continued.

electrocardiogram (EKG)

A test that records the electrical signals in the heart. An EKG is commonly used to detect heart problems and monitor heart status. Rachel had several EKGs throughout her treatment.

engraftment

The point when stem cells given to patient start producing new cells and growing a new immune system. Engraftment is usually defined by a certain number of new neutrophils in the blood. Engraftment was an important milestone in Rachel's transplant recovery.

engraftment syndrome

A condition marked by fever, rash, heart swelling, weight gain, liver and kidney problems, or swelling of the brain. It occurs at the time the new immune system is starting to produce neutrophils. Rachel experienced engraftment syndrome right before she was discharged from the hospital post transplant.

exacerbation

The appearance of new MS symptoms or worsening of old ones for a period of at least twenty-four hours. It is usually a result of a new area of demyelination, or loss of myelin, in the brain or spinal cord. Rachel had her last exacerbation when her treatment began and has not had one since.

Gilenya

A disease-modifying therapy thought to act by retaining certain white blood cells (lymphocytes) in the lymph nodes, preventing those cells from crossing the blood-brain barrier into the central nervous system. Preventing the entry of these cells into the nervous system reduces inflammatory damage to nerve cells. Rachel started this drug when it became obvious the A-B-C drugs were not helping her.

Hickman line

Also known as a Hickman catheter. A semi-permanent tube inserted into the chest and connected to the major artery at the top of the heart. It allows for easy injection of drugs and easy withdrawal of blood. Because it is a direct connection to the heart it needs to be sanitized every day, even when not in use. Rachel's Hickman line was not immediately removed at the end of her treatment because of a blood clot in her heart.

hollow bones

The term Rachel used to describe a long, deep ache in her bones. Rachel experienced this pain often enough that she developed a name for it.

infusion

A therapy delivered intravenously. During HSCT, Rachel's infusions were almost always through her Hickman line.

irritants, the

Rachel's term for a feeling like many little insects crawling under her skin. The sensation is a symptom of nerve damage. Rachel experienced this discomfort often enough that she developed a name for it.

lesions

Areas of the central nervous system that are demyelinated (stripped of myelin) or inflamed. They are detected through the use of contrast-enhanced MRIs. Rachel acquired fifty-five or more lesions before she had HSCT.

longitudinal medical trial

A study in which subjects are tracked over time. Rachel was required to return to SCCA annually for five years post treatment.

magnetic resonance imaging (MRI)

A diagnostic test that uses powerful magnetic waves to create detailed images of organs, soft body tissues, and bone. Rachel had scores of MRIs over the years and kept copies of all of them.

migraine

A severe headache, typically characterized by throbbing on one side of the head. A migraine is often preceded or accompanied by visual disturbances and vomiting. Rachel had these from an early age until she experienced hormonal changes during pregnancy.

mucositis

An inflammation of the mucous membranes of the digestive tract. It is one of the more painful side effects of chemotherapy. Rachel compared the feeling of mucositis to swallowing razor blades.

multiple sclerosis (MS)

A chronic autoimmune disease that affects the brain and central nervous system and can be disabling. *Multiple* means "more than one" and *sclerosis* means "scars," referring to the appearance of brains afflicted with this disease. Rachel was diagnosed with MS at the age of twenty-four.

myelin

The protective sheath that surrounds nerve cells and allows messages to travel through the nervous system. Multiple sclerosis attacks the myelin, and as the myelin disappears the signals being transmitted no longer reach their destinations. In Rachel's brain, there were so many attacks that in three spots there are permanent holes where myelin used to be.

myeloablative

A stem cell transplant done after a patient's immune system has been completely depleted through chemotherapy. Myeloablative HSCT is distinct from non-myeloablative HSCT, in which the immune system is only diminished. The myeloablative protocol has a slower recovery time but also a higher success rate than non-myeloabative. Rachel had myeloablative HSCT.

Neupogen

A medication that forces bone marrow to quickly grow and release millions of stem cells into the bloodstream. Rachel likened the pain from this to that of hollow bones.

neutropenic

Lacking an effective immune system. Neutropenic is defined as less than 1,500 neutrophils, or white blood cells, per microliter of blood. Once Rachel was neutropenic, it was not safe for her to be around crowds.

neutrophil

A short-lived, general-purpose white blood cell. The production of neutrophils is the accepted indicator that stem cells have established themselves and are functioning normally. Rachel's medical team monitored her neotrophil count closely.

non-myeloablative

A stem cell transplant regimen with a less aggressive combination of chemotherapy and/or radiation to prepare the patient for the transplant. The stress on the patient is less, but the success rate is lower. Rachel would have had this type of HSCT if she had been accepted into the Chicago study.

packed red cells

A concentration of red blood cells that remains after plasma is separated from whole blood. This treatment is given for anemia, especially chemotherapy-related anemia. Rachel received an infusion of packed red cells after chemotherapy.

phantom burn

A subdermal burning sensation due to nerve damage, sometimes described as feeling like acid under the skin. Phantom burning was the worst of Rachel's pain, but fortunately it rarely happens post transplant.

phlebotomist

A technician who draws blood for tests, blood donations, and research. Rachel had a blood draw by a phlebotomist almost every day while at SCCA.

platelets

A blood component involved in clotting. Rachel had platelets infused after her "birthday."

proprioception

How people perceive their bodies in space. Proprioception allows you to know where your foot is even when you can't see it.

Changes to proprioception were the first regular symptom that alerted Rachel to the fact that MS had affected her more than she had realized.

RBC

Red blood cells. Rachel had a bag of red blood cells infused after her "birthday," along with platelets.

relapsing-remitting MS (RRMS)

A form of MS with clearly defined relapses (also called attacks or exacerbations) that last for days or weeks and then subside. There may be full or partial recovery and no apparent disease progression between attacks. About 85 percent of people with MS begin with this form. This is the type of MS that Rachel had.

seasonal affective disorder (SAD)

A mood disorder in which people become depressed at the same time each year, usually in the winter. Rachel attributed her first MS symptom of depression to SAD before receiving her diagnosis.

secondary-progressive MS (SPMS)

A form of MS that often begins as relapsing-remitting but later becomes more consistently progressive with few or no relapses. HSCT has shown to be less effective in treating SPMS. Rachel was worried that her RRMS had progressed to SPMS before she had HSCT. Luckily that was not the case.

stem cell transplant

Also called a bone marrow transplant. In a stem cell transplant, stem cells are collected from the blood and stored. High-dose chemotherapy is used to destroy the cells in the body that are causing a disease. Non-diseased replacement cells are grown by injecting the harvested stem cells back into the body. Rachel's stem cell transplant was an autologous treatment, meaning the stem cells harvested and returned to her body were her own.

steroids

A large class of drugs with a specific carbon structure. The ones given to Rachel were similar to hormones the adrenal glands make to fight stress associated with illnesses and injuries. They reduce inflammation and affect the immune system. Side effects can include confusion, excitement, increased appetite, weight gain, nausea, trouble sleeping, thinning skin, cataracts, and cancer. Steroids are not prescribed lightly. In Rachel's case, steroids caused cataracts, but these do not affect her vision.

T-cell

A type of white blood cell that develops in the bone marrow and then migrates through the thymus to become part of the immune system. The job of these cells is to kill other, ideally harmful, cells. Prior to her transplant, Rachel's MS-affected T-cells were attacking her brain; post-transplant, her T-cells no longer have a memory of MS and the attacks on her brain stopped.

Tysabri

One of many DMTs, Tysabri is a laboratory-produced monoclonal (cloned from one cell) antibody. It is designed to hamper movement of potentially damaging immune cells from the bloodstream across the blood-brain barrier into the brain and spinal cord. Tysabri was the last DMT Rachel tried.

WBC

White blood cells. It was misguided WBCs that attacked Rachel's brain.